Woodturning
Projects and Techniques

Bruce Boulter

STERLING
PUBLISHING CO., INC.   NEW YORK

Published in 1987 by Sterling Publishing Co., Inc.
Two Park Avenue
New York, N.Y. 10016

ISBN 0-8069-6394-8

Phototypesetting by Photocomp Limited
Printed and bound by R. J. Acford, Chichester

Contents

Introduction

Many chapters in this book refer to the techniques of laminating or post-blocking and I would like to say a few words on the subject.

First, decorative effects can be obtained by lamination, either by using timbers of different colours, by defining outlines with fine veneer, or by taking apart any given piece of stuff and putting it back together again in a re-arranged form. The permutations are endless, governed only by the imagination of the turner.

Secondly, in a world of ever increasing prices the economy aspect of laminating cannot be overlooked. In bowl work as much as two thirds of the waste can be saved when producing a comparable size and style from the solid, indeed in Chapter 11 a saving in excess of 95% is possible.

Thirdly, some projects cannot be produced in any other way than by laminating, or even if they could the cost would be prohibitive. I would imagine a Tulipwood bowl of 12in diameter would be a rarity. I have never seen '*frutescens*' in such a size, and I shudder to think of the price even if it were available. However, if stuff 1in thick and about 4in wide is available there are several economic ways of making a bowl in such a size. There are many exquisite timbers derived from trees that do not grow to a great girth, and there are also timbers from trees that are so long in growing that the heartwood is invariably very degraded. Since large pieces are rarely obtainable, laminating, in one form or another, is the only answer.

I have sometimes, in a caption, referred to another elsewhere in the book. This has been kept to an absolute minimum and is employed only to avoid repetition and to save valuable space. Each project is explained to the very best of my ability and detailed in full. This method reduces the actual number of individual articles. However, several alternative projects using the same or very similar methods are suggested in each chapter. Since it is quite impossible to describe every technique or alternative method with each caption that accompanies a photograph, the reader is urged to read right through the book before starting any project. I have never subscribed to the theory that there is only *one* right way and, woodturning, like most crafts, is very individual. Turners often reach the same end by very differing methods, sometimes with different tools.

The readers of this book will be inexperienced, but they should not think that any technique is beyond them. Remember, there was a time when I thought so, but now I have experience behind me, yet there are still turning techniques I have yet to master. Disappointments and failures are inevitable, and the craft would not be worth tackling, and would be a complete bore, if each project went according to plan. Practice, experiment, and experience the sweet taste of success. You will be able to make better projects than are discussed here, so let this book be your guide only. Stamp your own personality on the articles you make.

We will study working safety at the appropriate time but for the moment I would ask the reader to consider *one very important point*. We will be using machine tools other than the lathe to prepare some of the components or to render timber to a working size. Some processes are repetitious and as experience and confidence grow, a casual attitude is inclined to develop. Complete attention and concentration is always an absolute must. There is no machine tool I know of that will jump up and bite you. To occasion an accident you have to do something silly: allow a bystander to distract your attention, let the mind wander to that pile of stuff in the corner that needs tidying, or just stop paying heed to the work in progress. Always *isolate the power* when changing or attending to saw blades, planner knives, etc, to make sure it is impossible for anyone to inadvertently activate the machinery on which you are working. Keeping a bulb burning at such time will indicate power cuts that can be most hazardous with any machines not equipped with N.V. switches. I will not pursue the subject further, as I feel it is the responsibility of makers to provide installation and working instructions with the equipment, and safety procedure can be obtained from your local safety authority. I would strongly recommend these pamphlets are not only obtained but thoroughly studied in your own interests.

Finishing will be discussed as we proceed, and as timber has a very irritating habit of sometimes containing defects, often not visible until some work has been done, I have included a chapter on how this can be easily overcome. Some may say with 'spectacular' effect.

I hope the reader will find inspiration and guidance from these pages. Take your time, attend to detail, stand back and reflect often, (when things go well as much as when not quite so well). Working with wood is an absorbing and sometimes frustrating pastime, but it is always a fascinating and intriguing study, allowing the worker great latitude in producing useful, stylish and graceful articles. Enjoy your woodturning to the full, and take care of your fingers.

Bruce Boulter.

Lamination work

There are many ways of producing decorative work in turning, using only a straightforward lathe, even of the most modest size or capacity. I would stress from the beginning that the following is by no means exhaustive. Neither do I profess to have any great skill or natural talent in the field of design, indeed I would suggest that if any of the pieces in the two photographs we are about to discuss were made in anything but timber there would be little to commend them from a design standpoint. But, by the simple expedient of mixing, varying or alternating the flow of natural grain, we are able to produce interesting and 'seemingly' intricate designs or formations. The reader will find all the techniques fully discussed in the following chapters. There is no great mystery, nor is it necessary to have expensive or complicated equipment with which to work. Most will be home-made.

All the following pieces under discussion are, with one exception, made of the same timber, but there is no reason for not using a mixture of timbers.

Fig. 1.1.   Lids. *Top left,* the centre, is plain side grain, a middle ring of twelve segment lamination with the grain running in a rotary formation, the outer ring is in radial form, bisecting the middle ring joints and the segments of the lamination are further divided by inserts of Ebony. The lid is known as 'capover' in style, with the edge rebated to fit a matching rebate in the body.

Top right, the centre, is of preformed block section, middle ring as before, outer ring of alternate rotary and radial segments. This style is 'inset', as the lid fits completely inside the body or box, and rests on a prepared rebate.

Bottom left, the centre is in plain side grain, middle ring of rotary direction, and outer ring with all the segments in a radial direction. The bases of all these have been laminated in a 'chevron' style. The timber used in all these examples is Andaman Padauk. They are lined with plastic inserts, insulated, and will be used as ice buckets or wine coolers. Finally, *bottom right,* in Swietenia Mahogoni, the nearest mahogany to Honduras, and a delight to work. The centre disc is of one piece halved to give a 'picture' or 'mirror' effect, outer ring in random segmentation but with a flowing effect that I was lucky to obtain. The base is again in random form, as I only had narrow wood to work with. It was therefore impossible to use a built-in formation to the blanks of either the lid or box.

Fig. 1.2. All four pieces are made in a timber that seems to carry a variety of names. It is Cordia Dodecendra, the more familiar titles being Grande Palisander or Mexico Rosewood, but not being a Dalbergia the term 'rosewood' is improper.

The box in the top left is from a plank ripped, bevelled and re-assembled in its natural form. The centre of the lid is *endgrain* cut in half, reversed and re-assembled (from the same length of wood from which the lids of bottom left and right are made). This section is let into a normal piece of sidegrain, and the outer ring is produced from a spare ring as detailed in Chapter 15 in mitred form. It is insulated and lined with a captive insert (Chapter 2). *Top right* is a pickle jar with a loose plastic insert. I will not dwell on its construction as this is covered fully in Chapter 2. *Bottom left* is a small box with a quartered lid of endgrain, set into a box blank before parting off, and *bottom right* is the same but set into a blank of heartwood to sapwood configuration.

Fig. 1.3. This is a board cut 'rift' or 'through and through' of a small log of Australian Osage Orange. The pencil line will indicate the edge in which we are interested, the one with the sapwood that is perfect along the entire length. This pencil line also shows that the edge of the plank is not straight; this is not really important, but would, if cut along this line, produce a blank that would have an imbalance in design. There is nothing wrong with that, as we are 're-arranging nature' (as this technique was once described) and anything that grows naturally will not have the sometimes desirable appearance of being machine made. I thought, however, this would be a good example to demonstrate how an almost uniform balance of design form can be achieved.

Fig. 1.4. As there was a little 'knuckle' on the right that could have caused problems, it was marked out and the balance of the plank divided into two equal halves. Then, using the inner line of sapwood as a guide, two further lines marked to join this centre line, which will produce two pieces of almost perfect symmetry as seen in Fig. 1.6.

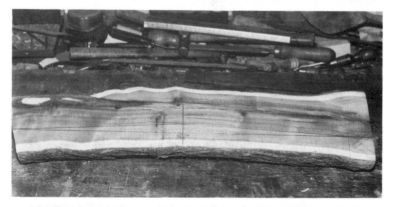

Fig. 1.5. Before the required stave was cut from this board it was turned over and the necessary material for the base was cut while there was still material wide enough to produce it. For this project, the operation was unnecessary, as it was to contain a smoked glass insert and the base could therefore have been produced from a different timber. This will of course reduce the width of the stuff to be used for the stave, but nothing is waste and my lace bobbin friends can make excellent use of small pieces of rare and precious timber. See Chapter 18.

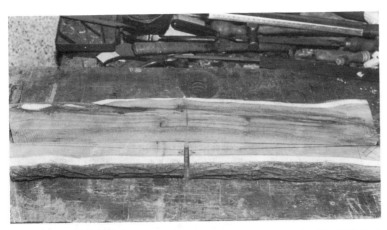

Fig. 1.6. The two pieces cut and the straightening out of the required piece can be seen. The sawn edge was then cleaned up with a plane. This 'face' will go to the fence of the circular saw in working the bevel. This means the sap/bark side would be bevelled first, producing a straight true edge. Then the stave would be reversed for bevelling the other side, explained in Figs. 2.1 to 2.5.

Fig. 1.7. The finished piece of twelve segment construction assembled in heart to heart, sap to sap, configuration. Note that the method used will render a finished piece that is greater in diameter than the available width of the board from which it was produced. There is also a lot of timber left from which the operation could be repeated, and still leave enough stuff for other articles.

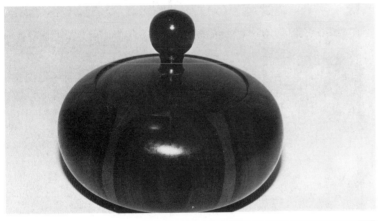

Fig. 1.8. An example in Ebony to illustrate how timber can be re-arranged to decorative effect. This piece is almost perfectly symmetrical.

Fig. 1.9. A complicated procedure is more easily understood if the student is shown what the work is *for*, before going on to explain how to use it, or produce it. Here we have one half of a log of Kingwood. Due to the presence of silica in the extreme heart I prefer to split such logs rather than saw them in the initial stage. This is usually a simple procedure as one only has to follow the lines of the shakes that will invariably be there. I then assess the size and shape of the stuff that will be produced from the available material, this is marked, and as will be evident I try to preserve a quantity of heart and sap. Of course not all timbers have such a marked difference between heart and sap; in some it is hardly noticeable. However, this format is by no means confined to expensive or rare timbers, for instance some pines have a marked distinction between the two, Scots pine for one, and of course Yew.

Fig. 1.10.   For a twelve segment lamination I have carefully arranged the segments to produce the best balance possible, and for the purpose of demonstration, numbered them boldly, but some form of numbering is a must or you will soon be in a muddle.

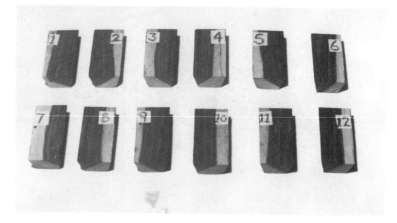

Fig. 1.11.   Using a suitable size of hoseclip, and obtaining the diameter required by first assembling the blank 'dry', the segments can then be assembled in numerical order. A flat surface is a must to work on, and it is important not to put fingers on the areas to be glued. Natural oils in the skin, not to mention mineral oils from honing stones, machinery etc that will inevitably be present on the fingers, will prevent a good bond being obtained. If the hoseclips of the right size are not available, several small sizes can be joined together.

Fig. 1.12.   When the segments are assembled and in order, the bottom clip can be *gently* 'nipped' up. *Do not overtighten*, as this will squeeze all the adhesive out of the joint and produce a weak bond. I think the reader will find with experience what is too much pressure. Think of any vise or clamp as a means of holding a given structure in place and apply pressure gently while the adhesive sets or cures. Vises are not designed to 'crush the work to death'.

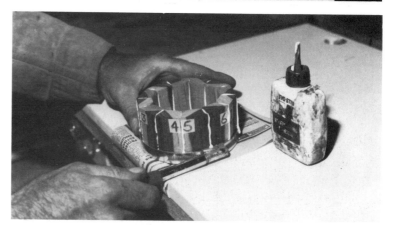

Fig. 1.13.   A second clip is placed around the top of the blank and equal pressure is applied. I have used a P.V.A. adhesive as it shows well in photographs. It is quite satisfactory, but for precious timbers like this, I would normally use either a phenolic or resorsinal adhesive. The blank must now be set aside to permit the adhesive to *cure* for the length of time specified by the manufacturers. Data sheets giving this information, and much more, can be obtained from most makers, and it is as well to have as much information as possible. A thorough knowledge of all the 'components' used is as important as skill with tools.

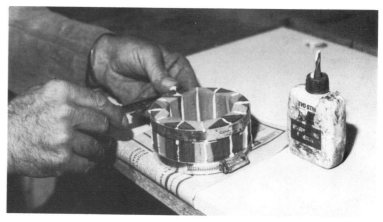

Fig. 1.14.   Before and after. These two were made from one length of wood which was cut into twenty-four segments to make two blanks of twelve segments each. Sort the segments out to provide as balanced a blank as possible. Here, the balance is almost, but not quite, perfect, yet still retains a natural look, I think.

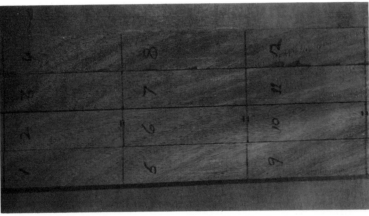

Fig. 1.15.   One of many other formations that can be produced is continuity of grain in a spiral pattern. By taking a given plank and ripping it to the required size, then replacing it, when sawn, in its original form, marking out and numbering as here. The staves can be bevelled ready to be cut into the required segments.

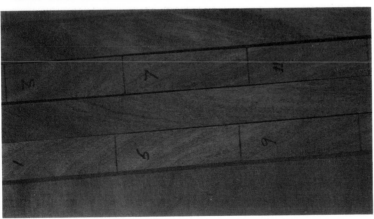

Fig. 1.16.   Alternatively, and using the same stuff as in Fig. 1.15, the staves can be reversed and a chevron design produced. From these two examples it will be obvious that (a) the form must be decided before the bevel is worked and (b) it is essential, having made the decision, to clearly number the pieces. Once the staves are bevelled they become directional, and will be usable only one way.

Fig. 1.17.   The same stuff used to produce a blank discussed in the previous figures, in this instance when the segments were cut. Re-arrangement improved the build-up from a design standpoint. A little time spent 'juggling' can pay dividends.

Lamination work with inserts

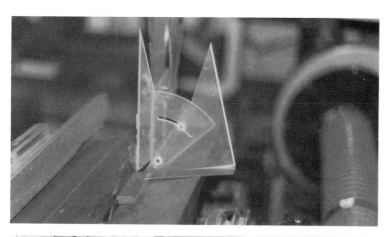

Fig. 2.1.   Having discussed the building up of staved blanks, we must now consider how best to prepare them. While some may prefer to use a machine planer, I find the surface produced from a sharp T.C.T. (tungsten carbide tipped) saw of *rip* type not only renders a satisfactory joint, but also a slightly less smooth surface, which gives a better bond. Power saws will vary in the provision for bevelling adjustment, mine is a touch 'hit or miss', as it has no micro adjustment. Here we see an adjustable set square, set to the required angle and, to ensure the set square is presented to the saw at a right angle, a small engineer's square supports it. Take care to keep the edge both against the saw and in between the teeth, or the 'set' of the teeth will cause an incorrect setting.

Fig. 2.2.   By easing the locking screw on my saw I am able to tap the table to provide the necessary angle. This can be a tedious business, but accuracy is vital, both for a safe blank to work, and for a good finished product. Having a lot of stuff ready ripped while the saw is in its right angle mode will be of considerable advantage. I have spent a lot of time obtaining the perfect angle only to find no stuff ready to bevel! If you only have one saw this can be most vexing.

Fig. 2.3.   As with many illustrations to come, for clarity I have set the guards out of the way. *Always*, whenever possible, use the guards provided, and, when ripping, the riving knife is a *must*. Ensure that the stave is in contact with the table at all times, when working the *second* bevel, as on narrow stuff especially, it can ride up the fence. Set the saw to approximately ⅛in above the thickness of the stuff used. Take your time *and use a push stick* for the final few inches.
MAINTAIN CONCENTRATION ON THE JOB IN HAND ALL THE TIME.

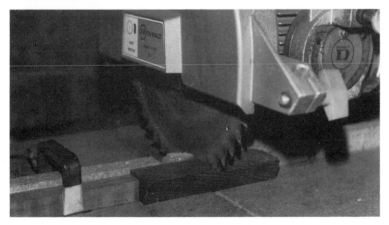

Fig. 2.4.   A close-up of the position of the fingers (I have had to lower the table for clarity). If the palm of the hand is kept in contact with the fence as shown, or a similar method is devised for your particular machine, this will both steady the hand and keep the fingers where they should be, out of the way of the saw. I repeat that this work can be dull and repetitive, nevertheless FULL CONCENTRATION IS ABSOLUTELY VITAL, ALL THE TIME.

Fig. 2.5.   A preliminary check can be made with a carefully set sliding bevel, but the best test for complete accuracy is to have a few lengths of cheaper stuff prepared. When the bevel is worked cut into the number of segments calibrated and assemble dry; if this is perfect all the rest will be, if not it's back to 'tapping' and 'testing'. They *must* be right. A magazine reader once wrote to me, "Following your instructions I prepared some timber for blanks. It was intended to assemble a twelve segment construction, but I must have got mixed up somewhere as they went together perfectly with eleven." How lucky can you get? It never happens to me.

Fig. 2.6.   A simple stop to ensure that each segment is of a uniform length, essential when assembling.

We now have a blank but with no means of working it as it has no centre or means of effectively mounting it between centres. Mandrels can be worked but such are not to my taste, I feel they are impositive and, to some extent dangerous. When the blank is forced on, as it must be, the wedge effect could cause the blank to split, and for this reason a tapered mandrel should never be considered. Many years ago I developed a jig which, since I first introduced it in an article in a woodworking magazine, has taken on the title of 'A BOULTER', and a commercial version, made by qualified engineers is also available. We will, in the following chapters, be discussing the variations of the 'Boulter' and, while the method of mounting the workpiece will vary, the basic principle remains the same. It is a positive, safe, and efficient jig for the sole purpose of accurately mounting a blank or 'centreless cylinder', to enable a flange to be produced into which 'something' can be placed. The 'something' will be either a base in timber for the type of blank thus far discussed or, as in the case of a picture frame, the glass etc, for clocks and barometers etc. In some instances, as the jig can also be used with solid timber, a considerable saving of timber will be achieved. For example, with the removal of the waste to mount a clock, the waste centre can be taken out for re-use. The 'Boulter' is, in the main, home-made, and used worldwide. It is, despite its 'bristly' appearance, quite safe to use provided a few safety precautions are observed and the jig is well made in the first place.

Fig. 2.7. A piece of 1in (25mm) good quality plywood, preferably 'marine' grade, but certainly 'exterior' grade, is attached to a faceplate. Do not use chip, particle, or blockboard for this one. Three slots are produced at intervals of 120°, and while four will be seen in a figure to come, this is merely for the making of small light picture frames where I use only two 'grips'. For all practical purposes *always use three*. As we will see in a moment, either a bolt with its head recessed into the rear of the plywood can be employed or, alternatively, a recess at the front can be worked. As I use this method a great deal and have several sizes of 'Boulter' it is worth the expense of a faceplate for each permanently attached. However, if the bolts, which are preferable to screws have their heads set in with epoxy, and the faceplate is identified with the jigplate, it can be removed and re-used for other purposes when the jig is not required.

Fig. 2.8. This is the cast iron version of professional manufacture, a delight to use although it weighs about 10 lb and when the lathe is switched off it takes a long time to stop. It is shown here with a blank mounted and the 'grips' in place. The hoseclip is a further safety precaution to prevent any likelihood of the grips being thrown out by centrifugal force. Though this is most unlikely to occur, the added precaution is recommended. Thumb screws and large washers, tightened without force (just as tight as is comfortable on the fingers) is all that is required.

Fig. 2.9. As will be seen here the grips, made from 'studding', i.e. pre-threaded rod of 5/16in diameter, are welded to angle iron of 1in angle and trimmed to a convenient or usable proportion.

Fig. 2.10. A further development of the 'Boulter' produced by engineers in Tasmania. The rear view shows a heavily ribbed casting with machined faces at the back of the slots, which will much enhance the positive locking of the modified 'grips'.

Fig. 2.11. The front face is divided by a series of rings. This will make the placing of the 'grips' a simple matter. The workpiece is then secured and, of course, centred with the Allen bolts. I have not at this time discovered what purpose the two threaded holes serve, but I could make an educated guess! Using this method all the pressure used to secure the blank is inwards. What could be better, or safer? The rule 'keep your fingers *your* side of the toolrest' still applies. This model was perfected by Mr John Still, who is not producing this jig, but would be pleased to loan the pattern for the casting to interested engineering companies.

As the turner must of necessity stand well clear of any projections when using it, the only danger is to bystanders. This applies to many machine tools, and the reader should realize this and take the appropriate precautions to safeguard children, pets, or any visitors to his workshop. Let us now discuss its construction.

Fig. 2.12. At the front of the 'Boulter' is the projecting bolt. This is only for the purpose of securing the disc, which will be worked to the diameter required to accept the given size of the blank. The life of these discs (plywood for preference) is considerable, as they can be used over and over again for progressively smaller blanks.

Fig. 2.13. The disc can be worked to size *in situ* with the long corner of a skew in the reverse way to Fig. 2.18 and if the jigplate is touched with the tool no harm will be done. This one has been in use for years. If using the steel jig, the fitting of a sub-face in timber would be wise, though the fitting of the centre-ring disc differs slightly, and this is not perhaps necessary.

Fig. 2.14. If the staves for the blank are of uniform length, and a snug but not forced fit is worked on the centre-ring disc, the blank should look like this when offered up. They don't always fit quite so well.

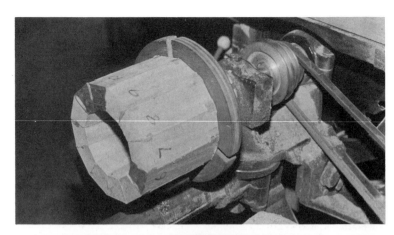

Fig. 2.15. The grips can now be attached and tightened with the thumbscrews, equally all round. Over-zealous tightening is both unnecessary and undesirable. They should be just as tight as is possible without hurting the fingers. Some people like to dip the ends in white or fluorescent paint to make them visible when turning. This is a good idea, but there are other ways of identifying them, as we will see.

Fig. 2.16. A hoseclip can then be attached for complete safety. Again it should not be overtightened.

Fig. 2.17. A different blank, of larger size, mounted on the jig. Note the marked line that will be visible when working and will indicate where the tool will foul the grip. I am using only two grips, but this is to demonstrate the jig. It is *always* best to use three.

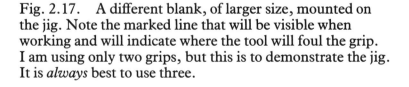

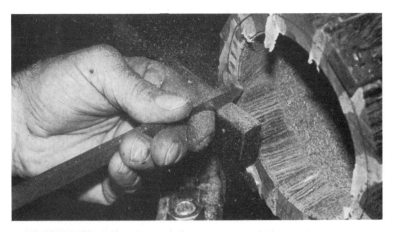

Fig. 2.18.   At a speed of approximately 1000rpm, certainly no faster than 1500rpm, and using a ¼in long and strong skew. With the toolrest set at a height that will permit the tip of the tool to work as near as possible on the centre line, i.e. toolrest height equals dead centre LESS HALF the thickness of the tool used. This will give the best working position. In practice any size chisel will do. I use a ¼in as only the tip is used, and as this is a 'coarse' action and the tip (long corner) won't last long, why keep sharpening a wider one? As with all work ensure that everything is secure and tight, and of course give the work a turn by hand before switching on. Keep yourself and your fingers your side of the toolrest all the time in working, and try to resist resting a hand on the work to hasten stopping when switching off. It could be very painful.

Fig. 2.19.   Apart from working a flange, for deep work some considerable section of the interior can be worked as well, another advantage of having a completely clear interior. Keep the long corner of the chisel sharp, it will be pushed away from the cut as it loses its edge. Once the size required is reached, or preferably one cut before, finish with a freshly honed or ground tool. Cuts of approximately ¹⁄₁₆in maximum will be fine for most timbers, extra hard stuff even less. One thick cut will be beaten by two or three thin ones every time.

Fig. 2.20.   The stuff for the base mounted on a faceplate and worked to a snug, not tight, fit for the worked base. I like to do the final sizing with a wide beading and parting tool. This section is, in most instances, best completely finished at this time. As in deep work it might well be most difficult to get at later.

Fig. 2.21.   What was once an unmanageable 'tube' is now a perfectly normal format upon which a variety of operations can commence. Remember: 'It is invariably easier to take a bit more off than to put a bit more back on' and, 'always measure TWICE and cut ONCE'. Over the past forty years my observance of those two rules has saved not only a great deal of timber, but a considerable amount of bad temper.

Fig. 2.22.   The timber in the blank we have been working is Grande Palisander (Cordia Dodecendra) from central America. This species varies a great deal from log to log in colour and density. It can be very soft or extremely hard. The grain will be found to be either ruler-straight or highly-figured, and it is a timber that can be full of hidden imperfections. Examples of the things we can make are biscuit barrels, pickle jars, jam pots etc. For some it will be preferable to have a removable insert so that the contents can be stored in a refrigerator without changing the container. In this figure the inside of the blank has been worked in exactly the same way as in Fig. 2.18 and the lip of the container/insert can be accurately marked for a really tidy, but loose fit. It may then be easily removed complete with its contents. Ideal inserts can be obtained in a variety of sizes from any store which stocks freezer containers.

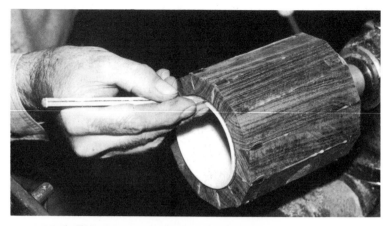

Fig. 2.23.   With the insert fitted, the base of the rebate to stop the lid can be completed, using the insert as a template.

Fig. 2.24.   With the lid rebate completed, a disc of plywood will support the work for reducing to a cylinder and for further styling. Note how little material has to be removed to effect the true cylinder in a twelve stave lamination.

Fig. 2.25.   Using the long corner of a very sharp, skew-shaped chisel, the top of the box is completed. The plywood disc will prevent 'spelch' and the tool will not be damaged if it touches the plywood. The other way of providing a clean cut top would be to complete this cut first and tidy up by working the lid rebate last.

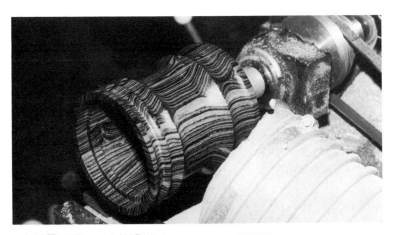

Fig. 2.26.   The finished box, polished inside and out, and ready for use. If you have a calculator you may care to compute the material actually used in this product instead of making it from the solid. It will be a revelation, taking no account of the saving in actual toil. Really there has been very little work to do.

Fig. 2.27.   Blanks can be used for a number of different applications. Let us consider one way of making an insert captive, as in, say, a biscuit barrel, or an ice bucket/wine cooler. Here we will be making use of a 'reclaimed' insert, i.e. one of good quality, sold containing foodstuff or similar. A 'sacrificial' blank is worked. It will be used to make components for various other uses. Here I have worked a collar to a given size to fit into a box of the same timber.

Fig. 2.28.   It is sanded and carefully cut off, worked as near as possible to the required size. A thin parting tool will be ideal as this will minimise waste. The sacrificial blank can now be set aside for further use, perhaps to produce a box or whatever.

Fig. 2.29.   With the box worked as in Figs. 2.22 to 2.26, the insert is fitted snugly and made captive with the collar. While straight-sided inserts have a distinct advantage, as they simplify fitting, shaped containers can add interest to the turning.

Fig. 2.30.   When the adhesive used to fit the collar is cured, the workpiece can be returned to the lathe for finishing.

Fig. 2.31.   This time the top or rim is trued up in the reverse order, using a narrow skew chisel with very light cuts. Note the 'spelch' mentioned in Fig. 2.25.

Fig. 2.32.   The 'spelch' or ragg occasioned by the previous cut can now be eliminated with the final cleaning up, cut and finishing. Take care not to foul the insert with the tool.

Fig. 2.33.   When sanding, try as far as possible to support one hand with the other for comfort and safety. For a square style finish as we have here, a cork block will give the best results.

Fig. 2.34.   Again for a straight-sided design a flat cork block is used to avoid any rounding over of the profiles, though the sharp arris edges should be very slightly removed. Allow the abrasive to do its work. Do not press too hard.

Fig. 2.35.   The finished piece, a biscuit barrel. While it is by no means always necessary to fit an insert, for food, tobacco, cosmetic creams, or anything sticky or moist, it will be preferable. Both the projects we have discussed thus far will be seen in Fig. 1.2, and both are produced in Grande Palisander.

Fig. 2.36.   The technique described in Figs. 2.27 to 2.35 will do for ice buckets but I prefer to insert the lining from the base. This also permits the insulating material (obtainable from wallpaper stores as 'expanded polystyrene insulating' material) to be accurately placed, and the inside of the blank to be sealed with sander sealer or similar to prevent moisture due to condensation. The blank is mounted in the jig and the entire inside to accommodate the lining is completed. It is not always easy to see or to be able to measure when working this way, but the job can be simplified by cutting the base of a sacrificial insert, keeping it as a permanent 'template'. The progress of the work can be controlled to a far greater degree as it will be possible to see what is going on as the work proceeds.

Fig. 2.37.   The blank being worked here is in Macassar Ebony, twelve segment heart-to-heart lamination. The depth being worked is about seven inches, so a long, strong skew is a must. The template is 'see through' so it will be a simple matter to complete the work to a high degree of accuracy. If the insert is to be a good fit and not wobble about or rattle in the box, this is essential.

Fig. 2.38.   When the inside is worked to a good fit for the insert, a further few cuts must be made to open the work to permit the insulating material to be inserted with the lining. The thickness of this lining material will be in the region of ⅛in, therefore only ¹⁄₁₆in will be taken from the working side. This final cut must be made with care to avoid problems and ensure a tight fit. Rough sand the interior and apply a good seal to the timber, and let it dry thoroughly.

Fig. 2.39.   Another method of making up a template, some may prefer to call it a 'mullet', is to fit a handle. There is a ply disc on the other side, and the template is, of course, reversable. We will see its use later on.

Fig. 2.40.   With the flange worked to accept the base, the blank is removed from the jig. The insulation is cut to a good fit and the plastic insert slid into position. Cold falls and heat rises, thus one thickness of insulation round the insert is enough. Two, three, or even more thicknesses can be applied to the base, both for better insulation and to compress the insert for a tight fit. Don't overdo it though, and test for fit dry, i.e. with the base piece.

Fig. 2.41.   When all is ready the base can be glued in position and the lathe used overnight as a cramp, or as in this figure a 'C' cramp or similar can be used. Allow the adhesive to cure.

Fig. 2.42.   The work can now be returned to the lathe for finishing. A roughing-out gouge is the perfect tool for a simple shape. Note that this one is being worked with no end support. (It never fails to fascinate me when working with ebony, from any country, why the heart is black and the sap cream to pink. Timber is indeed an absorbing subject).

Fig. 2.43.   The same cut again, from a different angle. The tool is held slightly down at the handle, and must be very sharp. Only the lightest cut is taken for the best results, and to avoid pulling the work off the faceplate.

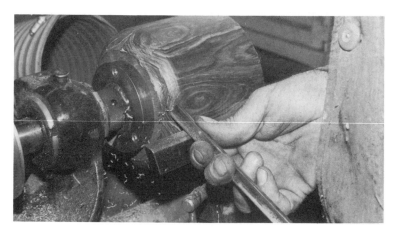

Fig. 2.44.   A blank in Cocobolo (Dalbergia Retusa) from Nicaragua and thereabouts, made as already described. The cross grain base can be blended into the sides in styling, but showing endgrain at this point should be avoided.

Fig. 2.45.   Sample inserts. On the left is a typical insert, in what I call 'soft' plastic, as the material is soft and to some extent pliable. They are inexpensive and freely available. On the right is the type that is less useful; it's still plastic but 'hard', brittle and unsuitable for our purposes.

Fig. 2.46.   If hoseclips are not available, you can make a larger diameter by setting two or more smaller sizes together. Indeed, as we will see later, this method has its advantages. Here is a 'Flexicramp' in use which is perfect for the assembly of larger blanks. This blank is in Andaman Padauk from, of course, the Andaman Isles.

Fig. 2.47.   The same blank set up in the 'middle size' Boulter jig. The slots are closed to give extra support and I am working with this large size with no safety hoseclip around the grips. This is again to demonstrate the equipment. A safety clip should ALWAYS be used. This is perhaps a fearsome size for those who are not used to this type of work, but in practice it will be found the larger the easier. Furthermore, the working method is shown better here due to the space available inside the working area. For this size, in this operation, a lathe speed of no more than 750rpm would be considered prudent.

Fig. 2.48.   A slightly tapered insert, tapering towards the base, inserted and ready for the insulating material which will have to be 'tailored' to fit. The remainder of the operation is the same as before. Again the point of interest is how little material and effort has been expended to bring the blank to this stage. In work of this size, some 9in diameter and perhaps more in height, a plywood base, or a cross laminated base, see Fig. 10.9, would help stability in a product that will part of its life be cold and damp as it contains ice, and be at room temperature when not in use.

Fig. 2.49.   Final shaping is the same as with the others we have discussed, though support with either the container's own lid or a disc of some sort is a wise precaution.

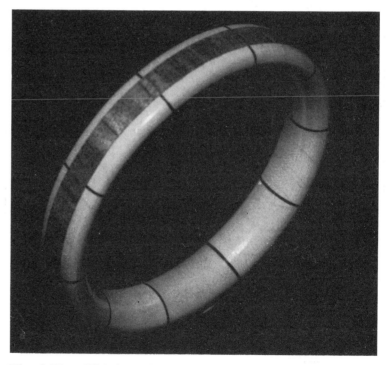

Fig. 2.50.   This bracelet, made by a friend of mine, is one variation of the techniques discussed so far. Made from a blank of Sycamore with an Ebony veneer inserted at the butt joints, then, following the procedure in Figs. 16.18 to 16.21, an inlay is inserted. Several such items can be made in one mounting, from one blank, and all but one surface or area completely finished before felling off.

Cutting and matching timber and lid designing

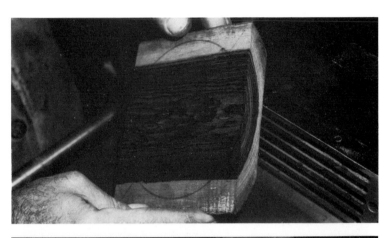

Fig. 3.1.   We must now turn our attention to the making of the lids or tops. There are many techniques, so we shall just look at a few! Let us start with a simple example of the use of solid, unlaminated stuff. Many people would throw this away, or cut the 'usable' figured heartwood away from the plain sapwood. I prefer to use the whole piece.

Fig. 3.2.   Cut the wood carefully into a disc on the bandsaw. Skiptooth blades are most suitable for turning. Three or four teeth to the inch, with plenty of set, will permit accurate and rapid cutting. These blades are especially useful for heavy work.

Fig. 3.3.   A hole right through the piece will permit reversal should the inside of the lid need to be worked. It is mounted on a single screw screwchuck.

Fig. 3.4. With the minimum of working it will be obvious where the 'art form' will be available. If the shape had been worked to a different style, a quite different formation would have been revealed. With timber like this you usually have only one piece unless you are very lucky, so it is worth spending a little time considering what it will look like after a particular shape is worked. Note the almost perfect symmetry at this stage. On reflection, that is where it should have been left, removing the balance of the waste after reversal.

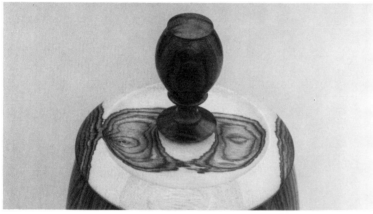

Fig. 3.4a. The close-up confirms this opinion. While the effect is still interesting, the balance has been lost.

Fig. 3.5. To see the advantages open to the turner in 're-arranging timber', the following will be an expansion on either 'shell veneering' or what the cabinet maker would call 'quartering'. There is no reason why the turner should not adopt similar methods with solid stuff. Left to right, we have first a quite unique piece. I must confess I have 'hoarded' this piece for some time, afraid to make a decision. Next is a build-up in a simple form, of sufficient quantity to 'cut and come again'. It is the section used for the centre of top right in Fig. 1.1. The lamination and the centring *must* be accurate for working. On the bottom right is a choice piece with a quadrant of sapwood. We will look at the applications of this format in a moment. On top is a build-up to be avoided, as the continuity of grain formation was not in balance over the length of the piece from which it was cut.

Fig. 3.6. In direct contrast we have a length of Kingwood (Dalbergia Cirensis) in almost perfect symmetry. The deep purple and black of the heartwood contrasting dramatically with the cream of the sap.

Fig. 3.7. With cuts of about ⅜in to ½in four segments are numbered and separated, using the thinnest saw available. This limits waste and maintains as close a continuity of grain formation as possible. The slight imperfection, the shake in the sapwood, will be of no consequence or danger in working later, as the lamination will provide all the strength required.

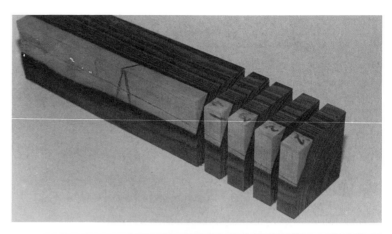

Fig. 3.8. The identifying numbers must now be transferred to the face of the segments. They are then arranged in the formation required and the first butting edge shot.

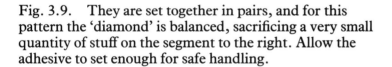

Fig. 3.9. They are set together in pairs, and for this pattern the 'diamond' is balanced, sacrificing a very small quantity of stuff on the segment to the right. Allow the adhesive to set enough for safe handling.

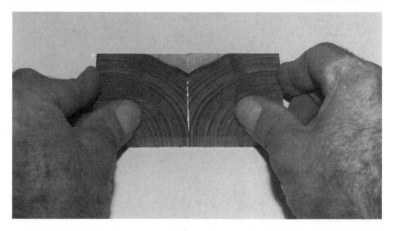

Fig. 3.10. The next edge to be glued is then shot in the same way on a shooting board, or in a mitre shoot if one is available.

Fig. 3.11.   The finished piece with an almost perfect symmetry, both in 'picture', the centre of the lamination, and in surrounding grain formation. This piece was used for the face of a clock. If it were to be worked, for example, for the tops of the boxes in Fig. 1.2 which are without knobs, the lamination can be glued onto a piece of backing stuff, carefully centred, and worked on the lathe to the correct size, inserted, and the waste piece turned off.

Fig. 3.12.   As the insertion of the normal tapered woodscrew would split laminations of this type we must replace the standard woodscrew with a 'setscrew'. A setscrew is a bolt with the thread over the entire length and a countersunk head identical to a standard woodscrew. As this chuck accepts a No.14 woodscrew, the shank of which is ¼in, a ¼in setscrew is compatible and of course fits perfectly, which it must for accuracy. The lamination we are about to study is abutted 'semi endgain', as it is a mitred construction.

Fig. 3.13.   The smaller chuck into which is secured the setscrew. A fibreboard (hardboard) washer is in place, both to keep the tool away from the chuck, and to defend the rear of the workpiece. The workpiece is *very* accurately centre bored, which is essential to maintain symmetry of the lamination in working.

Fig. 3.14.   A further washer is fitted, for the same reasons, and to provide plenty of grip, then a good sized steel washer, and the whole secured with a nut. Just a little more than finger tight will suffice. The work can now be turned to a cylinder.

Fig. 3.15.   Now we can take a normal piece of stuff mounted on a screwchuck in the usual way. A rebate is worked partway through, leaving just enough stuff to support the screw.

Fig. 3.16.   Measuring 'several times' and 'cutting as little as possible', and with the lamination supported by the end of the setscrew (the nut is behind it now) will both allow the woodscrew to pass through the hole in the centre, and also allow you to avoid handling the edge, as to do so would hinder adhesion later. If the timber is rare or expensive, and the practice is not taken to extremes, it would be possible to insert the lamination half way, and when the adhesive is cured, cut it in half to use the piece thus saved for another lid.

Fig. 3.17.   The chuck can be used as a cramp. Remove the outer workpiece from the screwchuck, drill ¼in and replace. Insert the centrepiece, replace the washer and tighten. The rear of the chuck flat and square to the setscrew surface will ensure the work is true. Allow the adhesive to set for handling.

Fig. 3.18.   As before a sacrificial blank is used and a rebate to accept the workpiece produced.

Fig. 3.19. The assembly thus far formed is glued into it. The limits to this build-up will be governed either by your imagination or courage, or perhaps prudence! Don't get carried away.

Fig. 3.20. We now have a lamination as described in Fig. 1.2. Indeed, this is the piece that forms the lid of the pickle jar in that illustration. It is separated with a narrow parting tool when the style is completed and a lid is the result.

Fig. 3.21. The alternative is to complete the box as seen in Fig. 3.20, and form a lid or top by working a rebate while it's whole, parting off, and fitting the top to the base while the base is attached to the faceplate/screwchuck.

Fig. 3.22. The rear or cut part of the turning will require finishing or further working, for which of course we have a perfect centring means.

Fig. 3.23.   The advantage of the setscrew method will now be appreciated, as it is simple to reverse the workpiece. Moreover, as the pressure is towards the chuck (on which will be a fibre washer) the entire inside right up to the screw is accessible. This is unnecessary for this application, as a mushroom pip (see Figs. 15.28–15.31) would be turned to cover the inside of the hole, but if both sides are to be seen in use this is a distinct advantage.

Lid production, built up method

Fig. 4.1.   The method discussed here will apply to the making up of preformed blanks for a number of applications, one of which will of course be bowls, or bowl shaped products. Here, more than ever, the safety aspect *must* be considered as this is a potentially dangerous operation. I believe there is no standard safety procedure laid down for the use of a mitre slide on a saw table used in this way, but the danger will be completely eliminated by the use of simple guards. These should make it almost impossible to get the fingers near the saw-blade at the rear of the jig, as this is where the greatest hazard exists. The block to the left protects completely the left hand, the dowl to the right makes it impossible to reach the saw-blade if the jig is used as shown. The angle is set with an adjustable set square, and the same cautions apply. Some people prefer to angle the jig in the opposite direction.

Fig. 4.2.   With the cutting angle set, the size of the block is determined by an adjustable stop. It is worth keeping the odd block to serve as a template and to save having to measure for a diameter of the finished blank, but such blocks should not serve for angle setting. They are not big enough.

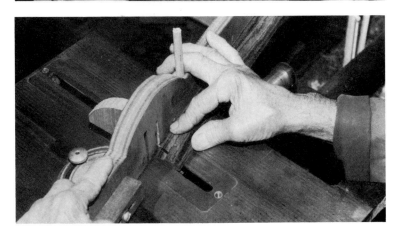

Fig. 4.3.   With the working stuff cut and planed accurately, the first cut will establish the angle. The stuff should be of uniform thickness. Width is not always so important, but for this project it is.

Fig. 4.4.   The required number of blocks can now be produced by a process of cut-invert-cut. The jig is pushed forward with both hands, the left is omitted in these photographs for clarity. Do not attempt to rush the work, let the saw do its job. Gently but firmly is the way to complete success and a good clean square cut. Again a TCT saw-blade is recommended, of crosscut nature. I do not like 'combination saws' for this work, I find they neither rip nor crosscut with the degree of accuracy I require for this type of work.

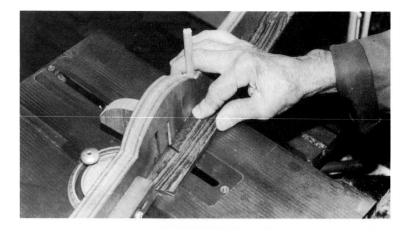

Fig. 4.5.   If a machine circular saw is not available, the work can quite accurately be effected by hand saw and shooting jig. If working with this method it is best to shoot *one* end of each block first, then move the jig towards the plane slightly, clamp it securely, and when the plane stops cutting each block will be of uniform size, which of course is essential. Do not make any adjustments to the plane iron by advancing or retarding it as this adversely effects the size of some of the blocks. It is therefore necessary to start with a well sharpened iron, finely set. If a large project in hard or abrasive timber is contemplated, start with some 'shims' under the plane, and by removing them one at a time, a new area of iron will be brought to bear. There will then be no need to re-sharpen during shooting.

Fig. 4.6.   Blocks for the mitre segment configuration in Chapter 15 can be cut and shot in the same way, with a slight modification of jig. It is unlikely the cut from a hand or tenon saw would give the degree of accuracy required without shooting.

Fig. 4.7.   Adjust the diameter of a Flexicramp with the blocks before any adhesive is applied. For a thin lamination such as this, a disc of ply or similar, of a diameter slightly smaller than the blank, is placed inside to bring the lamination to the centre of the cramp. This will centralise the work in the cramp.

Fig. 4.8.   A disc of protective paper is now placed inside to prevent adhesion to the spacing board, and the first ring of blocks can be inserted with adhesive applied to the butting surfaces only. It is as well to coat the cramps with wax furniture polish, as this will both ease the insertion of the final block, i.e. provide a slip, and make the removal of the glue squeeze that is inevitable much more convenient. *Take care with wax.* It is to prevent adhesion to the cramp; if any contaminates the work it will prevent adhesion there.

Fig. 4.9.   Adhesive is now applied to the top of the first layer of blocks in as uniform a layer as possible. A notched spreader is a useful tool for this, and the second, and if necessary subsequent layers of blocks, are built up in this order. It should be remembered that while the term Flexicramp is the name of this tool, it should be considered more as a 'former' or 'mould'. It has little actual cramping power, nor should it be used as a cramp in the full sense. If it is adjusted correctly in the dry state suggested, only a slight tightening will be required.

Fig. 4.10.   A further disc of paper is now placed on top of the lamination, then a further disc of ply/block board.

Fig. 4.11.   Light pressure can now be applied with cramps and the assembly set aside to permit the adhesive to cure.

Fig. 4.12. The lamination removed from the Flexicramp can be either cleaned up with a small plane on the bench for further work in the lathe, or one surface completely finished in this way to obviate the need to reverse when turning. We will see this particular lamination in use in a later chapter.

Fig. 4.13. Smaller, single layer laminations can be assembled with hoseclips. Always work on a true flat surface.

Fig. 4.14. An alternative method of centring work on the 'Boulter' jig has advantages for this work. The make-up at the rear is identical and the three slots are prepared. While any faceplate will do, if it's too big in diameter it will impede the use of the slots. About 3in diameter is ideal.

Fig. 4.15. Instead of a bolt to secure the centring disc, a small rebate is worked about ¼in deep and 2in diameter. The size is not critical.

Fig. 4.16.   A piece of ply is mounted on a screwchuck and turned to a diameter that will both fit the interior of the blank, (see next fig.) and with a spigot that will loosely fit the rebate in the 'Boulter'.

Fig. 4.17.   The hoseclip is still attached to protect the lamination from splitting at the joint. It is the lamination seen in Fig. 4.13 which is glued endgrain *only*, and overzealousness could cause splitting during the following operations. The centring disc is tested for an accurate, but easy fit.

Fig. 4.18.   The centring disc is set into the jig, so when the lamination is offered to it and attached to the jig with the grips, it will revolve dead true to centre.

Fig. 4.19.   Using the hole left by the mounting on the screwchuck, a woodscrew can be inserted to form a 'handle'.

Fig. 4.20.   When all the three grips have been secured, the laminated blank will be perfectly centred and the disc can be withdrawn, leaving access to the entire centre of the workpiece.

Fig. 4.21.   The centre can now be worked to a true surface. I have not used a further hoseclip with this small workpiece, but to do so is prudent. Even a length of strong string will do.

Fig. 4.22.   A homemade set square can be made up to fit the inside of small work, or small 'engineer's squares' are available. This method also lends itself to producing a template if the inside is to be 'stepped' or rebated.

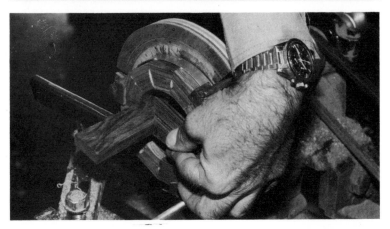

Fig. 4.23.   A piece of stuff is now mounted on a screwchuck either with a screw or preferably a setscrew. This piece is now worked as shown here with two diameters, as this will provide both extra strength to the mechanical strength of the joint and an increased adhesive area.

Fig. 4.24.   When working this type of joint in turning it is best to produce the *small* diameter in the female part and when this is a satisfactory fit, mark the larger diameter using the member as a template. Work to within a little of the marked line, and test several times for fit. As this piece will be on the top of the project and in full view it is worth a little trouble to get a good neat fit.

Fig. 4.25.   The lamination can now be removed from the jig and the other component glued into position. It is as well to leave the hoseclip on until the adhesive has at least set, preferably cured.

Fig. 4.26.   Now the assembly can be returned to the lathe and treated as a normal turning. In fact, in this instance, better than a 'normal' turning as there are no endgrain problems. The rebate method is again worked ready for the next or subsequent 'rings' to be assembled.

Fig. 4.27.   A further variation of the 'Boulter' jig method is displayed here. The only difference is in the way the centring disc is used, which is of larger diameter. A disc, bandsawn, is attached with a small woodscrew, and a couple of pins driven in, not completely, to prevent the disc moving in working.

Fig. 4.28.   The disc is worked to a size to fit the work as before.

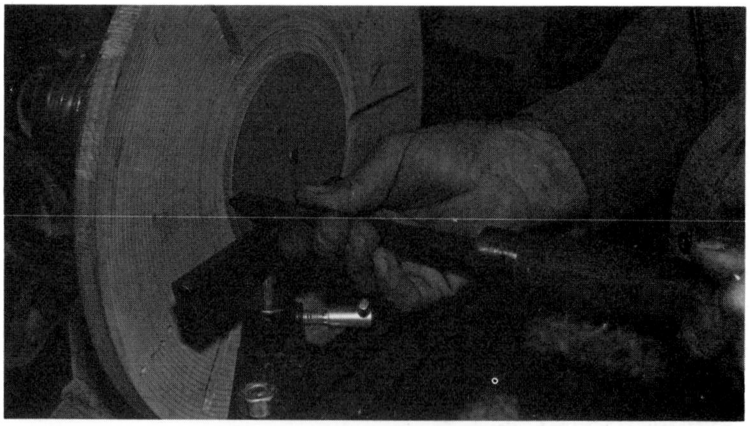

Fig. 4.29.   The workpiece is again perfectly centred.

Fig. 4.30.   The disc can now be withdrawn either with the fixing screw, or by pulling the heads of the pins, after securing the grips.

Fig. 4.31.   Similarly, the rebated section can be produced.

Fig. 4.32. The previously worked section can now be used to determine fitting. The procedure can be continued *ad infinitum*, though a degree of prudence should be exercised, and peripheral speed of the work as the diameter increases *must* be considered.

Fig. 4.33. With the assembly set up in a screwchuck using the setscrew method, the turning can be treated as a normal piece of stuff and can be reversed to shape or style the inside. Figs. 4.31 to 4.33 are the lids in Andaman Padauk shown in Fig. 1.1.

Use of faulty timber, endgrain spindle turning and bungs for shakers

I am bound to include a chapter or two on what might be called 'the behavioural tendencies of timber', as we all know it can be unpredictable, vexing, and at times, most tedious. That is, of course, why we like it. Every piece is a challenge and no two are alike. 'How do I know when a piece is ready and stable enough to work' is a question I am often asked. The straight answer is 'you don't'.

The ideal site to store timber is in a well aired and constant-temperature environment, stacked with an air gap of at least ¾in between the planks. Few of us will have this facility, so we must buy as we need or, if we have a stock or 'hoard' it will, of necessity, be kept in the open. If so, keep the top at least covered, do not restrict air-flow, separate with 'sticks', and avoid placing in the direct rays of the sun. It is as well to 'endcoat', that is to *seal* the ends of planks, especially if purchased fresh sawn. The petrochemical companies market products for this. For the shorter and more manageable pieces, dipping in hot wax will also go some way to preserving timber, or minimising end-splitting. Take great care with hot wax, it will scald like hot water, and worse, it will *stick* to you while it scalds. Timber can be considered as a sponge full of water; the easiest place for the water to get out is at the ends or at the endgrain. It also is the quickest exit, and this will considerably degrade the rest of the piece and, in its haste to evaporate, will split the end of the piece. This evaporation must be retarded as much as possible to permit a slow process throughout the length of the plank. The 'rule of thumb' is that timber will dry at the rate of 1in thickness per year, but this cannot be relied on. Moisture meters can be used, but in my experience are not to be relied on with stuff of the thickness the turner uses. A very simple method as an alternative is to weigh the sample, or individual piece, note the weight, and write it on the sample (or devise some elaborate alternative). When re-weighed at intervals of one month, in the case of fresh sawn stock, the rate at which the weight diminishes will be found astonishing. When the weight eventually stabilises it can be assumed the timber is dry. I have used the term 'assumed' quite deliberately, as it will be appreciated that if stored in the open the 'dry' state will correspond with the surrounding situations, a damp garden for instance. As most things made in timber will, for all practical purposes, be used in the house, if a product was made and finished in this 'dry' state, deformation of some degree or other could be expected, in fact guaranteed. It is therefore, good workshop practice to bring the stuff to a m/c (moisture content) that will match the finished surroundings. The stuff is brought into the workshop and the weighing procedure continued. To weigh a plank of say 12ft × 12in × 2in would be difficult and beyond the scope of the average kitchen scales, but a sample piece, say 2ft long × 6in wide, sealed as indicated, would be both manageable and capable of being weighed on the average domestic scales. The same applies to stuff purchased dry or 'ready for use' for working, if your stock is 'managed' in the way suggested, stuff ready for work will be available in some form of rotation. In short, a sound knowledge of the material in which we work is just as important and necessary as good quality equipment.

We must study some ways of dealing with the inevitable imperfections that will be found in timber. Some will be visible before starting a project, some have the irritating habit of making an appearance just before or at finishing. Some people discard a piece that is seen to be imperfect, but no one wants to reject a piece that has seen some work or effort put into it. While the examples I have selected could be described as 'severe' or, as in the final sample, 'gilding the lily', I have chosen both to lay emphasis on a subject that is difficult to describe, and certainly will be a matter of individual taste. Hopefully, I will be able to combine several stimulating ideas.

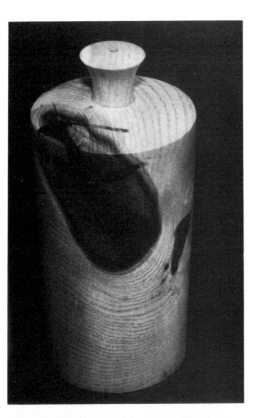

Fig. 5.1.   A salt shaker in Ash. Its wall thickness is ⅛in and the salt is retained by the use of a rubber bung in the base. It is in one piece, but its initial mounting in the lathe was of unconventional mode. Ash could never be described as an exciting or interesting timber – or could it? This close-up shows the piece finished and heavily filled; from this first sight would you bet on which is natural and which is repaired?

Fig. 5.2.   Some spices need to be kept airtight and while they can be purchased in suitable containers I prefer to produce my own and this Elm shaker is made in the same way but a Hornbeam lid fits snugly to the top. I then know, for example, that in an Elm container with a Hornbeam lid I will find the garlic salt!

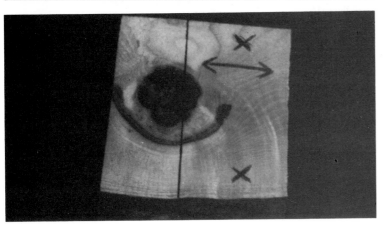

Fig. 5.3.   I used the term 'unconventional' but, in effect, this piece is to be cut for mounting in the same way a bowl would normally be turned, but this format will render a finished piece in the reverse to the 'norm'. The side or long-grain will be at the top and base and the endgrain will be the main feature almost all round in diameters of this size. Added to this we have a knot to deal with, the nature of which may or may not be a problem when we cut the section for working. It will be seen from the waney edge, punctuated by the arrows, the way the grain runs, and usually this would be the direction in which to convert this piece for working. We won't do that however, and the 'X' marks indicate the ends for mounting between centres.

Fig. 5.4. Thus mounted, there is a most unpleasant imperfection to deal with. It will, however, transform what might be described as a bland piece of Ash into a spectacular finished piece, if all goes well, and of course, if the style appeals. No special tools or tool angles are required for this format, and the square is reduced to a cylinder with a roughing out gouge.

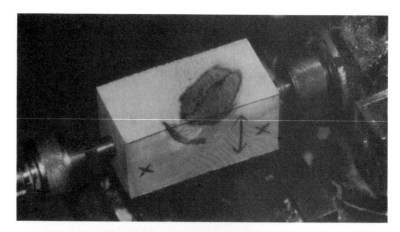

Fig. 5.5. The cylinder is cleaned up with a skew to assess the treatment necessary, and if the knot is sound within the timber and, indeed, if the work is worth proceeding with. I thought it was. It is accepted that the following will perhaps be a lot of trouble to take on such a piece of inexpensive timber but if the piece were an exotic section it could be both expensive and very rare.

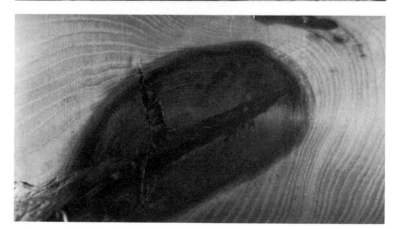

Fig. 5.6. The imperfection in detail, one end broken away completely and the knot deeply fissured, but quite sound within the stuff. Had the knot itself been loose it could have been removed and replaced with an adhesive.

Fig. 5.7. I decided to complete the rest of the shaping on the body of the article, before filling, with a freshly sharpened skew chisel, taking very light cuts. Note the finish behind the tool. Sanding is not my favourite pastime, and sanding on endgrain is to be avoided at all costs.

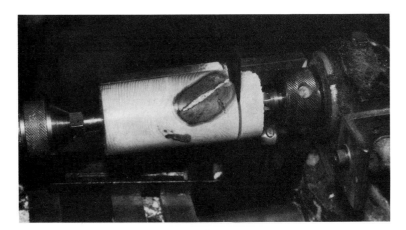

Fig. 5.8.   The broken area was worked down to perfect stuff (another way of dealing with imperfections), so a parting tool was used to determine where the perfect stuff commenced and, at the same time, leaving a fixing for a piece of timber to be inserted to provide a stopped square edge to fill, or work up to. As most of the interior was to be removed later, there was little point in wasting expensive epoxy filler. So the fissure was stuffed with shavings and well tamped down. This left a depth of approximately ⅛in to be filled. The medium I use, having tried other fillers, is epoxy (Araldite), either fast or preferably slow setting. The mix will be according to the maker's specifications; there are no advantages whatsoever in increasing the quantity of either adhesive or catalyst. Once mixed, it can be 'bulked' if necessary with fine sawdust or coloured, as in this instance, with poster paint powder. Add either or both to the mix a little at a time to obtain the desired result. With practice, exact matches in colour can be obtained, though there is an argument for a contrast in filling.

Fig. 5.9.   With the mix prepared, and using a stick of convenient shape and size, the filler is well pressed into the area to be repaired. The lamp method (see Fig. 12.28) can be used here, and will serve two purposes. First, the heat will thin the filler and render it more penetrative, and if the heat is maintained it will cause the filler to bubble and this can be an advantage. When the filler has dried, if it is rough sanded, indents will be found and these can again be filled with a toning mix to either produce a 'spectacular' effect (e.g. black filler with white dots) or just take the plainness away from the filled area. Other methods will be to score the filler just before it dries, and carry out the previous technique, or, as here, leave two small areas low to complete with a colour to tone with the white of the timber.

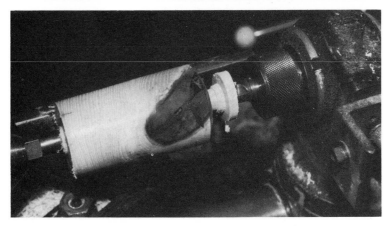

Fig. 5.10.   When the initial filling is dried but not necessarily cured, rough sanding will reveal any further attention necessary. Note the two areas I left to fill with a different colour, one on the arris of the top, the other in the centre of the main fissure. There are a couple more not clear in this figure and I have also roughed out the extreme top to see if any further attention is required there.

Fig. 5.11.   The workpiece is now completed and finally sanded, and only the top detail has to be worked. The turning can henceforth be treated as a normal piece of stuff. This type of filler is extremely hard. It is workable with tools if required, but hard on fine cutting edges. It is permanent and provides structural strength to a workpiece. Let us now continue with the turning.

Fig. 5.12. The jig discussed in Chapter 16 is used again here to advantage, but I will mention a few cautions. As this piece was of slightly tapered shape it was held (gently) into the chuck with the tailstock to maintain alignment. A double hoseclip, even treble, would make for more positive centring, acting like an engineer's chuck. The pencil lines on the chuck indicate the extremes of the 'contents', i.e. you can't see inside the chuck and to disturb the work in progress is not a good idea. The two 'blemishes' seen here are perfectly natural within the timber. Most people who inspect this piece for the first time think it *these* that are the repaired areas. Interesting, is it not?

Fig. 5.13. An auger or sawtooth bit will make short work of the waste removal. Ensure it is marked for depth, or a piece of 'Ash piping' will ensue! Such a configuration could have a number of uses, serviette rings perhaps, or a sleeve to cover another timber for subsequent decorative work. A flange approximately ⅜in deep is worked at the extreme base to accept the bung piece.

Fig. 5.14. As the rubber or plastic bungs that are available do not come in a variety of sizes, we must compromise if we are to produce the style, shape, or size project we want. A piece of stuff (contrasting timber is attractive for this purpose) is worked between centres as seen here. The dowel flange is not mandatory, but as the alternative would have been to alter the i.d. of the chuck, the flange was easier.

Fig. 5.15. With the workpiece securely centred in the chuck the o.d. can be turned to fit the rebate in the base of the shaker. A vernier will establish the size of the bung, and in this mode the hole can be worked with a tool if an auger of correct size is not available. For some bungs this method will present the possibility of working any profile that would otherwise be difficult to get at. When felled off, the bung piece is *reversible*, if required.

Fig. 5.16. The bung piece is drilled with an auger then a very slight dovetail profile worked. The widest i.d. goes to the *inside* of the shaker, rendering a positive hold on the bung.

Fig. 5.17. The finished ring felled off with a parting tool and ready to be glued into the base of the shaker. This method is obviously ideal for repetition and will have a multitude of other applications.

Fig. 5.18. The piece is inserted and glued and to all intents the work is finished. The mandrel is worked to fit the hole in the base and will serve to mount the workpiece again if any further styling is required or for a progressive finishing process such as lacquer (that will require sanding between coats). The production of the hole from which the contents will pour is seen in the next figure, though such a single hole could be produced in the drillpress, in the chuck, or, as here, with the revolving centre replaced with a drillchuck.

Fig. 5.19. By shaping the mandrel as shown, access to all parts of the workpiece is possible, including the rim of the base, for finishing. The bung piece should be set in slightly more than thickness of the rim of the bung to ensure the shaker sits flat on the table.

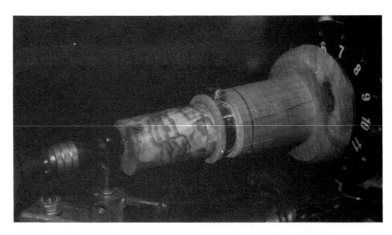

Fig. 5.20.   To conclude this study I have been guilty of 'overdoing it a bit', but only to make the point. This figure shows the efficacy of the dividing disc used in conjunction with a drilling jig to produce a concentric series of holes in the top of this shaker. Such a timber needs no special treatment from me, it is exquisite in its own right, both in colour and graining. This figure shows one side of a most unusual grain formation, and again you are looking at *endgrain* as it was mounted in the same way as the Ash shaker.

Fig. 5.21.   The other side of the piece in close-up, and a close view of the chuck used to complete the work. Note the fascinating contraflow of grain, which might be described as a carved effect. Such can be the effects achieved by showing as much endgrain as possible, and there are many so called bland or uninteresting timbers that can be brought to life using this method. It is also a format I like very much for the production of lidded boxes and small nut bowls, and this method of holding the stuff in working lends itself to the process both for a box and lid, not to mention bracelets, rings and so on. This figure also shows that the chuck can have a number of different diameters to hold work of differing sizes.

While it is quite outside the scope of this book to indulge in the problems of the environment, or for that matter to indulge in world politics, it will be patently obvious that the purchaser will have, to a greater or lesser extent, an interest in the raw material used by the woodturner. The following comments will, I am sure, occasion the odd eyebrow to be raised, or strike as much fear into the heart of the reader, as I experienced when the following facts were made known to me.

In every minute of every day 100 acres of tropical rain forest is destroyed, and much goes without the effort of re-afforestation leaving behind giant dust bowls, i.e. desert, where nothing will *ever* grow again. If the present trend continues without being checked in something like thirty years, it is estimated that half the life/species we know today will have been rendered extinct. Genetic material for uses in the production of food medicines etc. will be gone for ever, and something in the region of one billion people will have lost their livelihood. Sobering facts, that induce me never to waste even the smallest piece of this wonderful and 'renewable resource' – TIMBER.

Laminating with narrow strips and block laminating

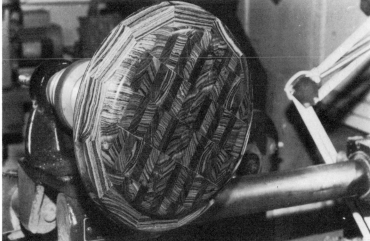

Some turners suggest that the technique of laminating should be considered as a way of using up bits and pieces of so called 'scrap'. I never consider *any* timber as scrap. It is a degrading term for a material which gives both the worker and the user great delight. I doubt if you would like any of your work, for instance a chess pawn, to be so described, as that made from a tiny piece of stuff much smaller than some would call scrap. Moreover, I would suggest the efforts we have studied so far could not be termed as made from anything but carefully prepared stuff. The term 'stuff' is an old fashioned worker's way of indicating 'the material out of which something is made', now more often called 'wood'. It is differentiated from 'stock', i.e. your hoard or tree. No one ever makes anything with 'tree'. The system gets a little confusing internationally, as the Americans for instance call stuff 'stock'. All that being said, the technique or practice of laminating can open up designs and will offer the opportunity for the turner to make good use of sections otherwise of little use in the lathe.

Fig. 6.1. Turnery for the table is always acceptable, and this cheeseboard is no exception. Made entirely from sections left over from a previous turning job, its endgrain centre set into a ring or frame of side grain, produced in Chapter 4 makes an attractive piece that is also functional.

Fig. 6.2. The finished piece showing the polish that can be obtained with natural oil.

Fig. 6.3. A pile of thin section stuff, by no means useless to the turner though on the face of it limited? I don't think so. The timber was planed to a uniform width; thickness is of no importance for this project. In fact, as we will see, one width *should* be of differing thickness. It so happens that in using this particular stuff it was of reasonably uniform thickness anyway.

Fig. 6.4. With the stuff so prepared it can be laid out on the bench, and by studying the endgrain, can be adjusted to make interesting patterns. If you are using several different timbers, a design form can be assessed or created. Try to avoid handling the surfaces to be glued as much as possible, but certainly keep the hands free of oil, wax, or anything that will hinder adhesion. Silicon sprays that are popular today for making the parts of the lathe slide smoothly are death to good adhesion, no matter what adhesive product is used.

Fig. 6.5. An even spread of adhesive is required, and the sashcramps prepared to size working as quickly as possible. Some adhesives start to set very quickly, more so in a warm workshop. Nip up the cramps, do not crush. I make this point, difficult to actually describe, what is nip, what is crush? If it is appreciated that the pressure that can be applied with cramps is considerable and will, if taken to excess, squeeze all the adhesive from the joint. At the same time we don't want a glueline a ¼in thick! It's a question of nipping about as hard as you would turn off a tap with a good washer.

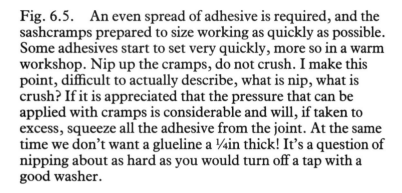

Fig. 6.6. Two further cramps are placed on top of the assembly to equalize the pressure, and the whole is set aside to cure.

Fig. 6.7. The glue squeeze can be removed with a long handled scraper. I find it easier and quicker to sharpen a scraper than to do the same to a plane iron, and some adhesives are hard on edge tools.

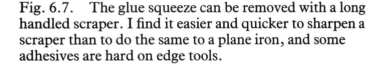

Fig. 6.8.   The lamination must now be planed and worked to a dead true size *all round*. It is vital that it is thicknessed accurately. It is common practice to use a lubricant with Bailey planes in particular. Generally, a little tallow or candlewax will be employed, to provide ease in use. The area of the lamination we are working on will be the next to be glued, so if it is contaminated little success can be expected. I always clean the sole of the plane with white spirit before this operation.

Fig. 6.9.   The prepared lamination can now be cut into 'slices', and a piece of protective covering used to stop contamination of natural oils in the handling during sawing. In the foreground are the slices as cut, and I have marked with an X the extra thick member mentioned. In this build-up, all the joints are in line, and this could be left so. However, by inverting, the design form is enhanced as will be the strength of the lamination.

Fig. 6.10.   With the alternate slices so reversed the 'brickwall' effect is produced, and this should be the way this work is laid up if a backing plate is not employed. It is worth numbering the parts or slices especially if, when cut in this way, something very complicated or interesting is revealed. It's very easy to get the parts mixed up during the next process.

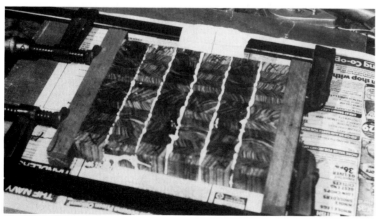

Fig. 6.11.   The lamination is assembled with adhesive and set aside to cure. Considerable strength will be available due to the multi criss-crossing of the grain in all the segments in all directions, further aided by the brickwall lay-up. It would be quite in order to work on the lathe in this form, provided due care was taken when fixing to the faceplate. You would be fixing into *endgrain*. However, by the end of this book I will have demonstrated several other methods in which turnings can be safely supported in working.

Fig. 6.12.   Were this piece required to be left in the square it could now be finished both sides with a hand plane. This is hardly likely in our case. One side, however, must be trued for either the application of a plywood backing, as we will be doing, or to mount on a faceplate in the lathe for further shaping. This work is best done with a small block plane, very finely set, and scalpel sharp, with a clean sole.

Fig. 6.13.   The number of cramps used here is to equalize the pressure and ensure the whole area of adhesion is equal. A piece of good quality ply should be selected.

Fig. 6.14.   When the adhesive is cured, or at least thoroughly set (24 hours for most), the work can be 'X' marked, bandsawn to a disc and a faceplate attached. Indicated with the pencil is the extreme of the rebate to be worked. If the lamination is of reasonable size, don't discard the corners removed by the bandsaw. They can be most useful (see Fig. 1.2).

Fig. 6.15.   With the lathe speed at about 1000rpm the rebate can be commenced. I use a ⅜in beading tool for this sort of work.

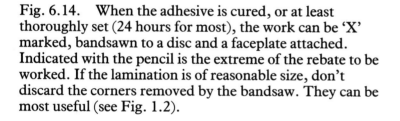

Fig. 6.16. With the depth of the rebate established, cut a line round the periphery with a chisel. This will be the shoulder of the joint to the ring or frame that will be attached in the finishing process.

Fig. 6.17. Finish with a narrow skew chisel using the long corner. To ensure a 'hairline' fit this rebate can be undercut lightly by one degree or so. If required the frame can be sited as in Fig. 17.16.

Fig. 6.18. We have discussed the production of a frame in Figs. 4.27 to 4.33. It will be clear from this photograph what is the advantage of a wooden 'Boulter' or the facing of the professional version, as it is necessary to work the centre right through to the jig. This can be done with complete confidence, though care should be taken not to damage the jig face more than is necessary. With a little practice this will be possible.

Fig. 6.19. With the centre piece, as it has become, still retaining the faceplate, (if it has to be removed for other work while the adhesive is curing, mark it; the faceplate has identical markings made with a centrepunch). It is glued to the frame and a few weights applied to make a neat joint.

Fig. 6.20. The entire assembly can now be returned to the lathe for final finishing. There will, of course, be no endgrain to worry about in working the frame and while this could be effected with a gouge, I am, here, using a very sharp scraper, half round shaped, to work a cove on the base of the piece. This will make lifting it in use that bit more convenient.

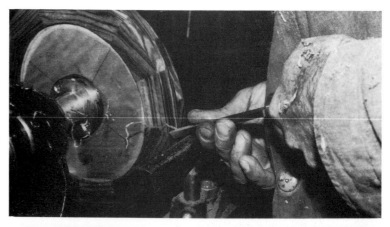

Fig. 6.21. Working an identical cove with a gouge on the top of the frame.

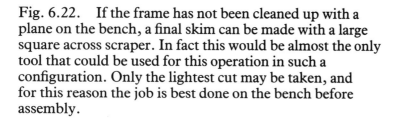

Fig. 6.22. If the frame has not been cleaned up with a plane on the bench, a final skim can be made with a large square across scraper. In fact this would be almost the only tool that could be used for this operation in such a configuration. Only the lightest cut may be taken, and for this reason the job is best done on the bench before assembly.

Fig. 6.23. The all endgrain face of the centre section can also be skimmed with a very sharp scraper and only the most gossamer cut made. We don't want to reduce the work any more than we have to, and it should not be necessary if care was taken in laminating-up.

Fig. 6.24. Again a half round gouge is used to soften the periphery of the endgrain centre section. Being both hardwood and endgrain, and to some extent short grain, it is of a brittle nature. I find the lightest stroking with a sharp scraper of this shape preferable to what may seem the more obvious tool to use, a square across.

Fig. 6.25. Sanding endgrain is not much fun, so the best finish that can be obtained with a tool is necessary. For final polishing, Danish oil is a favourite of mine, but although the makers assure me it is quite safe to use for work that will come into contact with food, I have not found this to be the case. I now use only corn oil in the finishing of articles that will come into contact with food. The corn oil is applied several times to well permeate the work, left to dry, and then buffed with a clean cloth or as here, with shavings. General maintenance thereafter follows the same procedure. In an effort to practise what I preached on pressure in cramping, I underdid it a little in the second stage of laminating the centre piece.

Split-turning methods

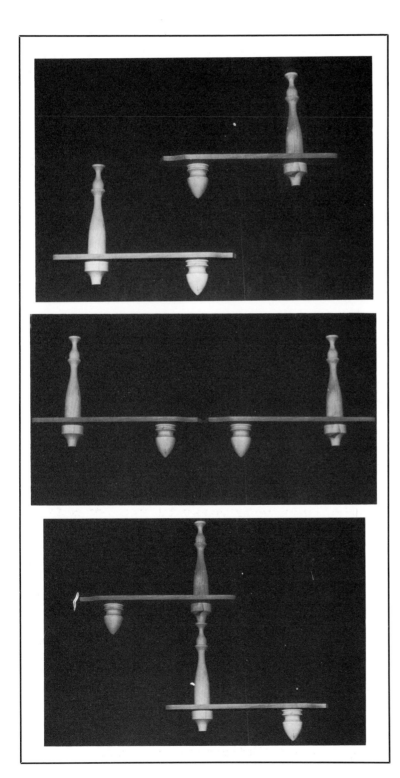

Split-turning is a subject that is often glossed over, and as the applications of this form of work are so wide and varied, I felt bound to include a chapter on the subject.

Fig. 7.1.a,b,c.   A set of simple shelves, *all* made on the lathe, and identical, but of a design that can be interpreted in at least three different ways. We can add to this the production of brackets on which to hang any number of things such as plates, flower pots, walking sticks, pots and pans, coats, hats etc. This is also an ideal medium for wall lighting. For the turner who also produces flatwork we will be able to discuss the manufacture of templates for 'general' use, or to use with a machine router. Such templates will be absolutely symmetrical, and worked between centres (that is of course why they will be symmetrical). I recently made for a builder a number of brackets to support a 'freeze shelf' (the shelf that runs round a room approx two feet down from ceiling). As there were a lot to produce I made the corners, *all sixteen* of them, in one turning. We will discuss this method. The flat brackets were produced eight at a time. The builder was amazed how quickly they were done. 'It's all in the fingers', I said.

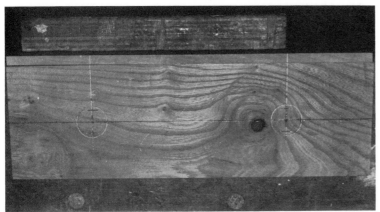

Fig. 7.2.   Let us commence our study of split-turning with the production of some small shelves. We will make them four at a time and I will mention the alternatives as we go. The first rule with this work is that the stuff *must* be accurately centred. While applying to all aspects of the technique, it is of paramount importance when making just pairs. So long as the centre section is square, the rest of the work must assume symmetrical proportions. We will not be using any adhesive and brown paper; such is not a method I care for, and we will see it has its limitations. Here we have the centre piece, hardwood is preferable, and if the working template which will be formed is to be retained for future use, hardwood is a must.

Fig. 7.3.   The same centre piece is also used to lay off both the fitting points of the shelves and as this will indicate where the holes for this purpose will be it also serves as a template or 'rod' (an actual size drawing) for the holes for the screws that will hold the turning together while working.

Fig. 7.4.   The stuff for the shelves must be accurately prepared in thickness and with one square edge, width is not so important. For the purpose of clarity here I have used a few different timbers. However, for this type of article mixing timbers should preferably be avoided.

Fig. 7.5.   Here we have the assembly ready for turning. Figs. 7.7 to 7.12 will make its construction more clear. Supported by the two lathe centres is the centrepiece, each side of which are the two shelves. This is covered by two 'flanking' pieces (not mandatory, but should be used to start this method with until experience is gained). This may seem, on the face of it, a lot of timber to use, and to waste, for the production of four small shelves. I think not. In the first place the whole can be used as many times as you like to produce the same configuration, and it can be used to produce a different configuration, albeit smaller. As we will see the centrepiece will hardly be touched with the tool, thus it can be used for other work and as we will see later, the 'flanking' pieces could be used as separate entities in their own right. Moreover a few pieces of fibreboard or ply could either be slipped into the assembly, or used as flanking pieces, and perfect templates for a router be provided. The centrepiece could also be ripped and thicknessed, and would also provide either a bracket plate or template. Thus, little or no waste is occasioned.

Fig. 7.6. In turning, the assembly assumes all the aspects of a normal between centres job, and no special techniques are either recommended or needed. Lathe speed will be as normal work.

Fig. 7.7. This close-up of the uneven end being turned also serves to indicate the content of the assembly and the ease with which it is turned. This 'scruffy' end was left so quite deliberately to make the point. Tidiness is, however, of the essence, and more often than not takes no longer than a slothful approach.

Fig. 7.8. With the shaping complete, sanding is possible with the lathe running but, as such a small area requires sanding, it is just as easy to complete the work stationary. Note the pencil mark round the work to indicate the presence of the screws; this is a wise precaution. The use of brass screws is recommended, but a steel screw is used first to prevent the possibility of the brass screw breaking.

Fig. 7.9. In the previous figure the toolrest is set up to the work in the correct working position, i.e. where the tool would be in contact. It will be seen from this figure that it would be more difficult indeed to strike the screws in normal working. Furthermore, they are countersunk for added safety. We also see here the two shelves completely finished with no need to work nearer the drive centre than can be accomplished in perfect safety. The tailstock end is identical, and a ring or cup centre, preferably revolving or live, should be employed.

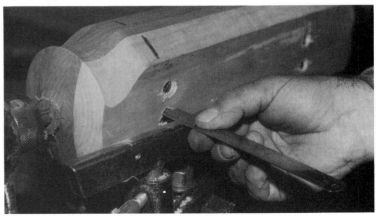

Fig. 7.10.   The assembly dismantled. The profiles of the shelves are compound, which cannot be achieved with a machine router as the cutter will produce an identical moulding of necessity. One use for the 'flanking pieces' would be the backplate of a pendulum type clock. The screw holes being covered by the clock, pips, supports etc. The centre piece is hardly worked, and is returned into stock. Alternatively, the whole can be used as a former in its own right to reproduce the same shelves as often as required.

Fig. 7.11.   We will need to fix the shelves to some form of bracket, and as this bracket is also made in the lathe, we can employ the fixing method to remove the screw holes in the shelves. There will obviously be no need to mark a centre line, as it's already there when the two shelves are lightly cramped together. A sawtooth bit is used to work the two half round housings, but whatever bit is used ensure it does not force the joint apart on entry. The diameter of the drill is immaterial as long as it just removes the screw holes.

Fig. 7.12.   The four completed shelves can be finished and polished. Try not to get polish in the borehole as this will impede adhesion later when the work is assembled. The shelves can, of course, be used either way up or either way round. It is also interesting to note the number of other forms such an assembly could take, with the pairs adhered together for instance to make a type of étagère with doubled pillars instead of the usual four. It would of course be far simpler to have produced the four shelves from two pieces of stuff, ripped into four on completion. This would effectively remove the two screw holes (see Figs. 7.13–7.15) in each pair. However, this method shows what can be done with small pieces of stuff, or if for any reason it was necessary to work in this way.

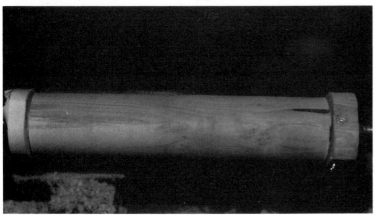

Fig. 7.13.   The brackets are really straightforward split turning. My aversion to glue and paper jointing is manifested in this case as in the finished work the section in one part is thin and delicate and would be subject to fracture if forced apart. Furthermore, I question the safety factor. Two pieces of stuff are screwed together, with the screws placed in the waste material at the ends. Note the masking tape at the headstock end to identify the 'no go area'.

Fig. 7.14.   Stuff for split turning should not be X marked in the usual way. A measurement taken to find centre *along* the line of joint will ensure the two halves will be precisely placed between centres. The turning can be worked to the desired style, and the housing for the shelves produced with precision. We will study this later. The whole can now be finished completely, save the small area at the extreme ends.

Fig. 7.15.   These ends can be turned quite thin to obviate the need for too much hand finishing, or finished off with a disc sander. See the comments with Fig. 7.33.

Fig. 7.16.   With the two components brought together and glued, the whole can be cleaned up with a small plane. There will be no 'goo' to clean off. The small bracket is worked in the same way, and if several are required a number can be produced in one turning. The hole for the smaller bracket in this style could be 'stopped' when drilling, thus not showing the endgrain of the bracket.

Fig. 7.17.   Other ways of making shelves can now be discussed. Perfect matching pairs will not just materialise; care in preparation of the stuff is important, as is accurate marking out. I feel it is as well to have not only a good bench upon which to work, but to have a modest set of bench tools, and some expertise in using them. A reasonable sized plane and a tri-square are among such tools.

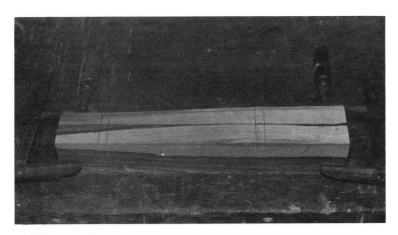

Fig. 7.18. The stuff is trued and marked out to indicate provisionally where the housings for the shelves will fit, in this style, top as well as bottom. This will be a good place to fit the 'keyhole' plates for wall fixing, as this will be in the widest part of the turning.

Fig. 7.19. The keyhole plates I use are of 1in in diameter, and a sawtooth or auger bit is used to produce a housing just deep enough to set them in flush. It will then be necessary to chop a short mortise to accommodate the head of the roundhead screw that will secure the fitting to the wall. All this work is completed before turning.

Fig. 7.20. The professionally produced cone chucks are a relatively new product and have a variety of uses. One drawback is they are only made in various sizes to accommodate stuff in the square up to about 2in or so, depending on maker. However, we will be making our own in a moment so perhaps this is not so important. The equipment comprises a cone to screw on the headstock as you would a normal faceplate, and a further cone, revolving, to set in the tailstock. If the workpiece is of too great a size in the square to fit into the cone the stuff can be chamfered either between centres (in this case it would need to be screwed together) or, as here, with a chisel on the bench to produce a fit.

Fig. 7.21. With the stuff mounted in the cones (the drive is of course friction, but no unnecessary pressure should be applied by the tailstock), the work can commence. If using square stuff in these cones there is a tendency for the stuff to slide in the joint while working. This can be prevented simply by placing a disc, the thickness of which is the multiple of the depth of the two housings for the keyhole plates, in the said housings.

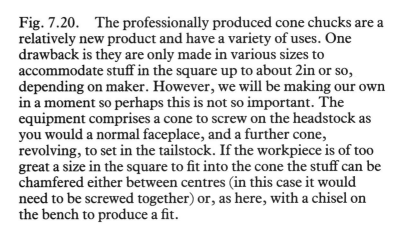

Fig. 7.22.   Using the actual shelf as a guide, the housing can be worked accurately. I use a narrow parting tool for this job. If these housings are completed first, any spelch in working can be turned out in styling.

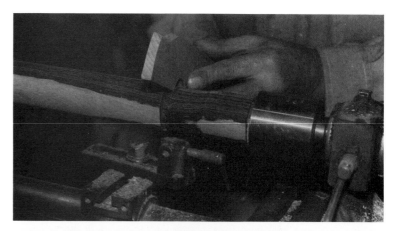

Fig. 7.23.   Two perfect half turnings produced in a pair that will also match in grain, or as near as is possible, by cutting the stuff used from one length and inverting. Complete with the shelf housings, all that is necessary is to finish the ends. As the finished product was to be oiled this was left until the whole was assembled. If finishing between centres, beware of polish in the housings.

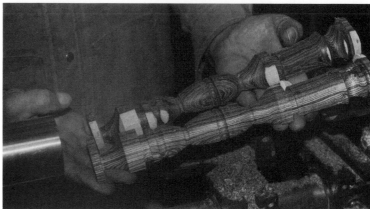

Fig. 7.24.   Another form of shelf production. From left to right, the centrepiece, the two flanking pieces, one with no holes visible for obvious reasons, and two worked and finished pieces. The extreme right was for use as a stand in another project, the feet of which will cover the screw holes, or to be more correct 'make use of them'. The remaining piece I have marked out for use in this project; the shaded area is removed after drilling.

Fig. 7.25.   A shooting board is a useful tool for the turner, and is used a lot in laminating. Here it is employed to ensure the sawn edge of the off centre drilled and ripped shelf is trued straight and square. A shooting board is necessary for this work if some experience in using a plane is not available, as the working is under control all the time.

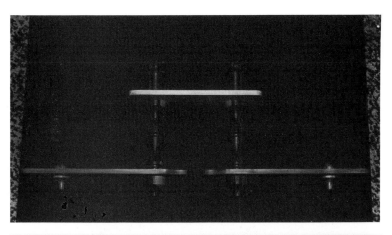

Fig. 7.26. Another style, finished with Danish oil. The small end supporting brackets have been worked to appear above the surface of the shelf. In all this the actual size of the work undertaken is governed only by the capacity of the equipment available, and experience gained with practice. Start with the smaller work first: spice racks, nicknack shelves, after which the sky's the limit.

Fig. 7.27. Home-made equipment for repetitive work. The reader may be wondering why I mentioned the number of corner pieces required for the freeze shelving in one room. All rooms, no matter what shape, will have four corners? Not so, as some rooms have alcoves, or recesses. This one did, so repetition, which I do not much care for, was necessary. I made up the following jig, and two faceplates were fitted with a hardwood as in this figure. A Stanley 'centre finder' is a useful tool to have for this job, and the fixing screws are of a gauge compatible with the size of the holes in the metal faceplate.

Fig. 7.28. Each of these two prepared pieces were worked, with identical recesses. Using the Coronet revolving centre set with the 'thread adaptor' as shown, one of the prepared cones could be mounted in the tailstock of the lathe.

Fig. 7.29. I now have what is more or less a cone chuck, but of much larger size than is available from the makers.

Fig. 7.30.   Four pieces of stuff 2½in square were prepared and taped together, for convenience of handling. They must fit the prepared chuck very snugly, and must also be of identical length. While I like, and would be the first to encourage, precision in any working, I am bound to admit the 'fit' here was a little more by *luck* than expertise. Nevertheless, the work definitely must not slop about.

Fig. 7.31.   One of the many advantages of this method is the rapid production of articles. Here we have eight corner brackets, made in two designs, all but the extreme ends finished in one turning. These were for an order for corner plant-pot brackets, bored in the lathe (see Fig. 12.27 for the arm and the fixing screw).

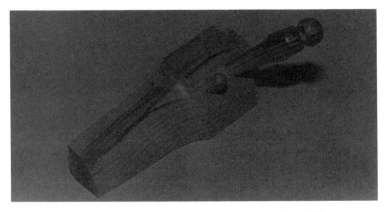

Fig. 7.32.   One of the finished corner brackets. The arm to hold the macramé plant-pot support is glued and the bracket is supplied with the dowel loose (to be fixed after screwing to the wall).

Fig. 7.33.   A few other styles for hanging various articles, all produced as split turnings. For every one seen here, one other was produced *at the same time*. Confirmation of my dislike of the glue and paper joint is clear. I feel if the work thus assembled were secure enough to work it would be of sufficient strength to possibly break the thin section in extreme left and right brackets as the two halves were forced apart. A final word of caution when split turning. When parting the work off, or parting down to clean up after removal from the lathe, you will have *two* sections to contend with. While a section of, say, ½in in diameter would be acceptable *on the work*, each half section will be a circle ½in at its widest, but only ¼in at its narrowest. This may not be of sufficient strength. The same calculation applied to *four* sections between centres would be quite unacceptable from a safety view point.

Using bottles and jars

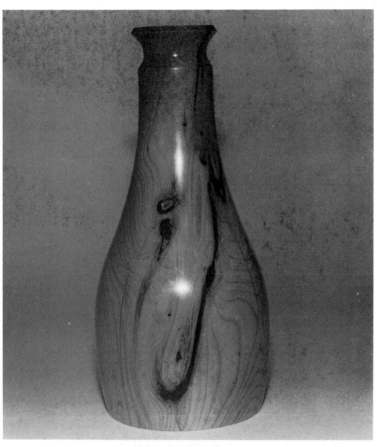

Fig. 8.1.   The range of attractive containers used by manufacturers to market their products is tremendous, and the sad thing is that these jars, bottles etc, usually find their way into the dustbin. While a range of containers can be obtained from turner's suppliers, I find a selection to meet most of my needs from the former source.

The method we will discuss in this chapter will capture the bottle within one piece of stuff, and in effect produce a vase. However, by bringing the bottle nearer to the top of the timber, covering and producing a stopper in matching or contrasting timber, it would become a dispenser for salad oil, vinegar etc.

Fig. 8.2.   As one of the techniques for holding work involves producing a straight sided hole in the base of the work of a size commensurate with the expanding collet used, for some applications a decorative finish can be employed. There are a number of ways of achieving this, leather discs, parchment with the name of the timber or maker (turner) either in pen, the 'rub on letters' of proprietary make, or, as in this instance, enamel discs on copper, available in a variety of sizes from art shops or those who specialize in supplying this craft. I find this not only covers, or to be more correct, fills the holding point of the turning, but to some gives the impression it was fitted for the sole purpose of adding decoration to the turning.

Fig. 8.3. With a piece of well figured, and slightly imperfect, Yew mounted between centres and worked to a true cylinder, the container can be offered up and any relevant sizing or design ideas can be marked in or assessed. Leave sufficient material to permit the working of the fitting for the chuck being used, in this project the 6-in-1 (old pattern). This is also a good time to investigate the figure or markings in the piece of stuff, and I keep the most interesting in the part that would be least worked, so not losing the rather dramatic black marking seen both here and amplified in the finished piece.

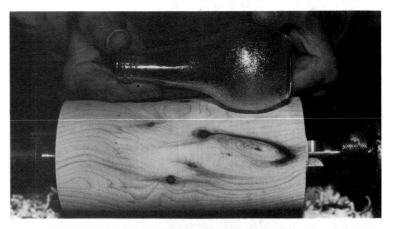

Fig. 8.4. At the tailstock end, which will be the top of the finished project, the fixing for the chuck is worked. In stuff of this diameter, i.e. greater than that which the chuck will accommodate, it is necessary to turn the area down to a size that will fit the ring of the chuck. It must also be of a length that will permit the split rings to be fitted.

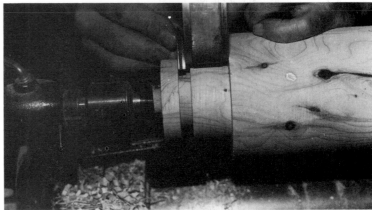

Fig. 8.5. With the workpiece securely fitted in the chuck and with some support from the tailstock, the end or base can be trued up, either with a parting tool or, as here, with a gouge as this will eliminate the need to sand the small area that will be left after hollowing.

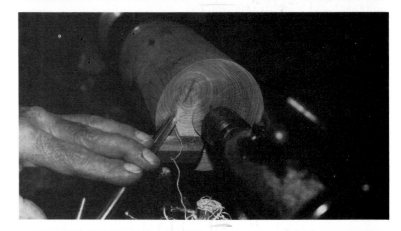

Fig. 8.6. The tailstock can now be fitted with an engineer's geared chuck, and most of the waste can be removed with drills of increasing sizes. At this stage only drill in as far as is necessary to accept the bottle, plus ⅛in or so.

Fig. 8.7.   With some timbers gouges can misbehave when working into endgrain. The long corner of a skew will work wonders if this is the case. Present it to the work in the horizontal or with the handle held four or five degrees down, at a speed of around 1000/1500rpm. The point of the tool will not dull too quickly, but it must be kept very sharp to render a reasonable finish, and as this part of the work will never be seen a fine finish is not required.

Fig. 8.8.   A half round scraper will also be found effective to work the bulbous shape required for this insert. The scraper used here is half round of hooked shape with a tungsten tip. They are available either for left or right hand working, i.e. inboard or outboard working.

Fig. 8.9.   Persistent checks with the insert will pay dividends. While a slight slackness of fit is required to allow for any movement of the timber and prevent it from breaking the glass, the less that is removed to accommodate the insert the more timber will be left to allow for styling the outside.

Fig. 8.10.   The interior is finished and is an 'easy' fit for the insert. It will not be permitted to slop about or rattle as we will see in a moment.

Fig. 8.11. A rebate must now be worked to accept the base disc. Again it should not be produced to a tight fit against the glass. By using a piece of stuff cut to fit the rebate, produce a tolerance of approx ¹⁄₁₆in according to size of project, (timber twice this size would require, say, ¹⁄₈in).

Fig. 8.12. With all the hollowing completed, and the rebate worked, the stuff can be removed from the chuck. The disc to close the base can be sized to fit. The base disc is held in the expanding mini collet chuck made by Coronet and is of 1in diameter. For thin work like this, I usually produce the fitting for this chuck/collet with a sawtooth bit of 1in diameter and to a depth of ¹⁄₈in fine. Test often for fit in this initial stage. As no adhesive will be used, and as this disc will be driving the workpiece, it wants to be very snug.

Fig. 8.13. The original workpiece is now fitted *dry* to the base piece, supported by the tailstock, and of course does not contain the glass insert at this stage. It will also be noted it is re-mounted in the lathe *reversed*.

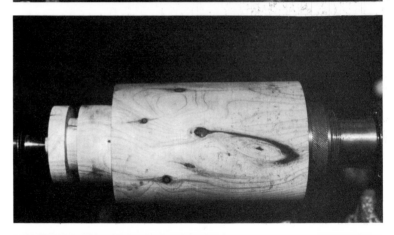

Fig. 8.14. A roughing out gouge would make short work of removing the waste to produce the required shape, but Yew is a delightful timber to turn, so I indulged myself with a new gouge made from HSS (high speed steel). Not only is the steel different but the shape of these relatively new tools is also different, inasmuch as they are produced from a true cylindrical shape of steel. They take a bit of getting used to, and what better way to try any new tool or technique than on waste.

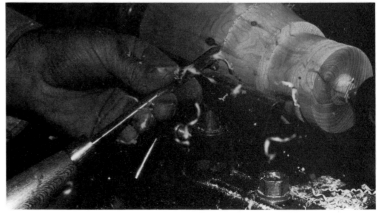

Fig. 8.15. It will now be obvious why the glass was not inserted and the base glued in position. The advantage of this method permits the vase to be removed once or twice to check dimensions. If the glass were inside, and you were unfortunate enough to work through the stuff, the dangers of flying glass would be presented.

Fig. 8.16. When you are satisfied that no further working will be required, other than final fine finishing cuts, the two sections can be assembled. Scuff the centre of the glass with coarse abrasive paper to provide a good key for the blob of silicone rubber 'caulk' that will provide a flexible but firm base for the insert in its slack fitting. The same treatment will be applied to the top or neck of the bottle. The base is then made permanent with timber adhesive, and when all is assembled there will be no rattling of the insert and the seal we have produced at the top will prevent liquid getting between the glass and timber.

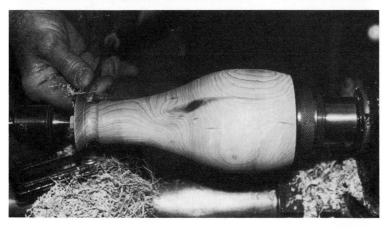

Fig. 8.17. With the adhesives given time to cure, the work can proceed and the vase be completed with sanding and polishing, supported all the time by the tailstock.

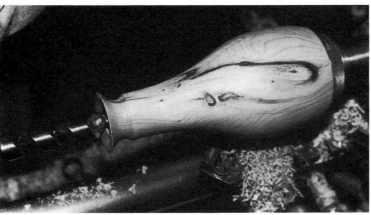

Fig. 8.18. The tailstock can once again be fitted with a machine auger, of a size just under the inside (i.d.) size of the glass insert. Running the lathe at its slowest speed, the final work can be completed. If plenty of silicone rubber was pushed up the inside with a dowel rod or similar, and as suggested placed round the neck of the bottle, a watertight seal will be effected.

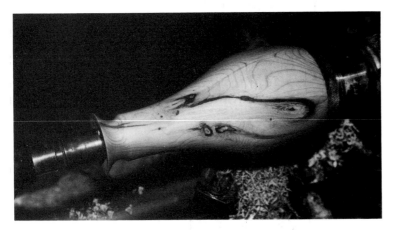

Fig. 8.19.   If it is necessary to return the work to the lathe, as for a progressive finishing process, it is a simple matter with the type of mounting used here and the work is supported by the tailstock fitted with a revolving centre.

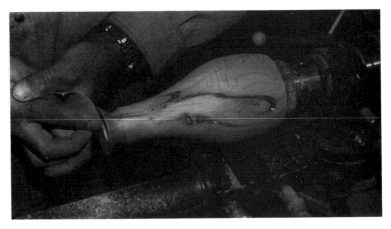

Fig. 8.20.   The tailstock can be withdrawn to permit access to the inside of the neck, for finishing and polishing.

Fig. 8.21.   An alternative to these suggestions would be to work a mandrel as seen in Fig. 5.18 on a screw chuck. Slide the work onto this mandrel and support with the tailstock. A revolving centre is preferable but, as the collet fitting will be covered by the enamel disc, a dead centre is quite acceptable. Remember, when sanding or polishing on the lathe always, as far as possible, support one hand with the other.

Fig. 8.22.   A selection of disc designs. With the base finished, and with a selected piece of stuff showing a balance of grain formation, the addition of the decoration puts the final touch to the work. The disc is glued with epoxy (Araldite) or similar.

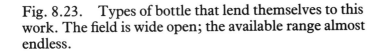

Fig. 8.23.   Types of bottle that lend themselves to this work. The field is wide open; the available range almost endless.

Wet wood bowl turning

Fig. 9.1. A technique that seems to be growing in popularity is the turning of 'wet wood'. Some superb effects can be obtained, as can a few disappointments if care is not taken. There are many methods and the practice could be described as an art form. Turners like Michael O'Donnell have taken it to this stage, and in my opinion some of his work is a joy to behold. One of the basics we can study here is the working of a log, of freshly felled Maple. This is a piece of limbwood from a diseased tree, as will be seen from the discoloured centre, and of course just what we want. On the left is the other half of the length I persuaded the forester to 'give' me, and the finished bowl which I regrettably flattened off. This was my first attempt at this technique, and the sequence was carried out with some degree of trepidation. Nothing ventured, nothing gained.

Fig. 9.2. The first essential is to produce a hole about 3in deep in the diameter to fit the pinchuck in the next figure. In this case 1in diameter using a machine auger in the drillpress. It is as well to get this hole as near dead centre as is possible to judge, both from the point of view of comfort in initial turning, and to retain as big a finished piece as possible.

Fig. 9.3. The 'pinchuck' we will look at in close-up in the next figure. Various makers produce this accessory to a basic chuck. There may be a temptation for the reader to implement a home-made device of similar nature made in timber. I would advise strongly against such an idea, the strains imposed are considerable as we will see.

Fig. 9.4. The principle of the pinchuck is simple. A flat is produced on a given diameter of steel cylinder in which a pin, when placed dead centre, assumes the exact diameter of the cylinder. The pre-bored stuff can then be placed on this cylinder with ease. If the lathe is then turned *by hand* and the work held firm, the pin rides up or across the machined flat and jams the work securely, as it is driven into the timber.

Fig. 9.5. With the log so secured, the method suggested in Chapter 14 could be implemented, but cutting on a bandsaw would be a hazardous operation as, at this stage, there is no flat to support the base. So, I set up the toolrest, carried out all the checks, and at a speed of approx 750rpm, using a ⅜in gouge, made a start.

Fig. 9.6. This operation is little more than normal roughing down of square stuff, in fact, easier. There are only two corners instead of four, and wet wood works like butter anyway. I took my time and with light cuts, frequently moved the toolrest in close to the work, stopping the lathe to do so, of course.

Fig. 9.7. The log was soon reduced to a more usual form and a recess worked in the end, which will become the base for the chuck that will be used to complete the project, in this case a small collet.

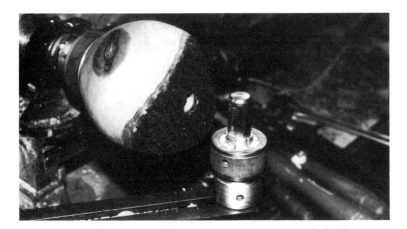

Fig. 9.8.   Reversed and secured with the chosen method of holding for finishing, this figure shows the pinchuck removed (revealing the hole which served to get us this far). By reversing the procedure in Fig. 9.4, the pinchuck can easily be withdrawn, although sometimes a little 'pulling' is necessary.

Fig. 9.9.   The hollowing out is normal procedure, aided by the initial hole. Some pinchucks are of 1½in diameter, so are not only strong but also remove a lot of waste before starting the hollowing. Wet stuff is easy to work, so it did not take long to rough out the waste and finish off with a freshly sharpened spindle gouge. I tried a scraper while I had plenty of stuff to work with, and it was an abysmal failure. I would imagine sanding could be a bit tricky on a very resinous timber, but in this case I started with 150g abrasive and finished with 320g soaked in teak oil.

Fig. 9.10.   The idea is to leave the finished piece as near to its natural form as possible. In some timbers the bark can be retained around the rim, which will follow the line of the outside of the log. In this case it fell off, leaving a rather rough edge. This edge must be finished by hand as, due to its shape, it cannot be done in the lathe. A belt sander, which I do not have, would be a useful piece of equipment to complete such pieces. It is, however, not necessary to have a complete log to try this technique. Half logs are most suitable, and would be mounted first with the flat outwards (i.e. the pinchuck set in the half round).

Large bowl lamination

Making bowls from the solid is a delightful job for the turner, and there is little doubt that some delightful effects can be achieved from a selected piece of stuff, if a study of the available material is made. There is also considerable scope for design and form in the laminating process; like everything it will depend on the turner's particular taste. The method of laminating is a tremendous saving in timber, and work for that matter. While the cost of adhesive must be considered, as must the time taken in

producing the lamination, for the turner who works mostly for pleasure, the latter will not be of significant importance, and the former will be certainly more than commensurate with the cost of waste from the solid, usually very much on the credit side. The drawings in Fig. 10.20 will indicate the saving in cost and effort, and only involve a disc. If the actual square from which a bowl is usually produced is considered, the economy is that much greater.

Fig. 10.1.   A relatively simple construction of twelve inches in diameter and four inches deep, made in Iroko. For the adventurous, as experience is gained, other constructions will suggest themselves. I saw one recently where all the segments were edged with veneer, vertical as well as horizontal. A bit too much for my taste, but nevertheless a most interesting and painstaking work. I would imagine the stuff was first veneered both sides of the flats, then cut into segments, as the blank was laminated. Either veneer was placed vertically in the joints, or the same way making rings individually, planing them flat and assembling in the usual way. Not really so complicated when you analyse it, but to the novice, all laminating looks ten times more confusing than it really is. This chapter will also give me the opportunity to introduce the 'frightener', it is the big 'Boulter', the one that causes a scattering of onlookers as I go to switch on. They soon shuffle back though, when they see how docile and *effective* it is. Rather like laminating, it looks far more fearsome than it really is, but it should *not* in any circumstances be used at a speed *above 500rpm*. It is the tool to turn a laminated blank into a finely finished bowl – all of the same timber, or contrasting if you wish, with the basepiece *inserted into* the work for appearance and for strength. It is infinitely more effective than the more standard method of attaching a lump of something or other to the base. While in this exercise I have used an ordinary cross laminated section of solid stuff in the base piece, there is no end to the alternatives available, using any of the techniques discussed in this book.

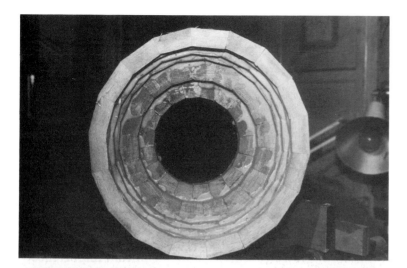

Fig. 10.2.   A blank of eighteen segments per layer, in six layers of differing thickness, to some extent pre-shaped in laminating. The degree to which you can take this technique will show in your bank balance at the end of the year!

Fig. 10.3.   The big 'Boulter' jig. Some twenty inches in diameter and made from two thicknesses of good quality ¾in blockboard. Not all this material is sound and flat, so buy the best, which will last forever. Mounted on the lathe and turned to a true disc. After the slots are cut, turning the lathe by hand and using the toolrest produces circles of differing colours approx ¼in apart. A felt tip pen is ideal for this job, and the different colours will prevent the lines 'running into one another' when you are trying to trace them round for the next operation, which is to place the three locating blocks. It would be possible to use the same method we have discussed before, but to use a disc of plywood up to 16 or 18 inches in diameter would defeat the economy we are looking for. Instead I use these three 'locating blocks'. The rough o.d. of the blank is measured and the blocks set to this measurement. By rotating the lathe by hand, it is a simple matter, by slight adjustment of the blocks, to set it turning true. The rear of the jig is seen in Fig. 10.13. The blocks are secured with nuts and washers.

Fig. 10.4.   Support the blank and apply the grips, still only held in place with wing/fly/thumb nuts. Only two are used; I have, over the years, found this to be quite adequate, as any sideways movement is prevented by the blocks.

Fig. 10.5.   While this assembly may appear 'formidable', I would stress the safety factors. With the blocks secure, no sideways movement is possible, and even if the grips did fail (which it is really up to the turner to see doesn't happen), with the toolrest up close and with the work revolving at approx 500rpm it would be impossible for the workpiece to jump out of the lathe. Again I use a ¼in l/s skew chisel to produce the required finish to the centre of the lamination.

Fig. 10.6.   The base of such a blank can be finished on the bench with a block plane. However, if just holding a tool up to revolving work appeals to you in preference to pushing a plane, quite a large area of the base can be cleaned up and even finished with a straight across scraper. In practice as there will be some shaping work after the basepiece is set in, little more than the immediate area around the centre hole will need any attention.

Fig. 10.7.   For the best work, and of course for strength, it is best to check constantly that the mating surfaces are square with one another. I find a small engineer's square very useful for this purpose. This is one way of ensuring the worked flange is true; the other would be to test with the stock of the square held inside against the jig itself.

Fig. 10.8.   The finished job, a flat flange with no rebate. For this style, a 'capover' basepiece, no rebate is necessary and the style will provide its own plinth. For a perfectly flat base, the basepiece could be fitted as in Fig. 10.14, and the rebated form would add mechanical strength to the joint aided by the increased adhesive area.

Fig. 10.9.   One can never have enough faceplates and, as my lathe has a device called a 'centre ejector', it was a simple matter to buy a few and have a *qualified* welder/engineer make up the faceplates for me. I mention this as owners of Coronet lathes might wonder what I'm using. There is also the possibility of the same practice being applied to other machines.

Fig. 10.10. Using whatever method is available for your particular lathe, the faceplate is centred and secured. I am using here two pieces of ⅜in stuff, cross laminated. While solid stuff could be used, this method not only greatly increases stability and adds strength, it also offers further means of decoration, and will permit the best possible use to be made of thin stuff.

Fig. 10.11. The centre piece is now worked to fit the centre of the blank. One half of the ⅜in lamination will enter the previously worked flange providing a shoulder, thus further adhesive area. The other half will be exposed to form the plinth, so it would be best to work this section to a finish at this stage, or at least, to a point where only sanding will be required. Any glue squeeze when the base is fitted can be wiped away with a damp cloth.

Fig. 10.12. With the base fitted, and indexed to the faceplate, in case the faceplate is required for other work while the adhesive cures. No attempt should be made to work until the curing process is complete, no matter how impatient you are to proceed. Note how, by adopting the 18 segment build-up even on a piece of this size, the pre-formed blank is almost a cylinder.

Fig. 10.13. If for any reason your lathe will not permit work to be carried out on the rear, or the shape required is one that cannot be worked after mounting in the normal way, considerable styling can be effected by the following means. The blank is centred in the 'blocks' (mine are of angle-iron with a bolt welded on, but wooden blocks with a bolt through would serve the same purpose), and using the grip slots in the jig the blank can be secured with woodscrews and washers. It is necessary to determine the position of the screws in relation to the waste, so the screwholes will be removed in styling.

Fig. 10.14.   A blank worked as previously described. The double rebate will permit a flush base to be fitted. The outside is completed, and sanded up to the top layer of lamination. It is most unlikely this would ever need to be done, but the facility is there nevertheless.

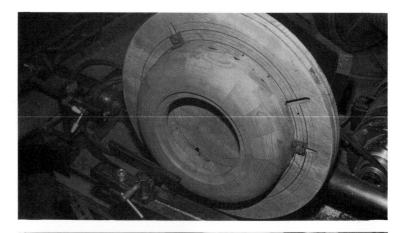

Fig. 10.15.   I believe it is suggested by the makers of the Flexicramp that only a scraper should be used to complete work of this nature, and I'm sure they have their reasons for the comment! However, I would suggest that with modern adhesives, and so long as the pre-formed blank has been produced with care, no hazard is present. Moreover, I would further suggest that with the multi crossing and recrossing of grain the strength factor is considerably greater than with solid stuff, that may contain an imperfection not visible at commencement or during working. It is, of course, quite possible to complete this work with a scraper, and as there will be an absence of endgrain a very acceptable finish can be expected. I prefer to employ a cutting tool. First, I remove the uneven exterior, here with a standard ⅜in bowl gouge; a similar size or larger spindle gouge would do the same job.

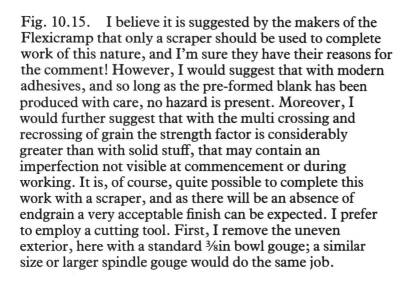

Fig. 10.16.   Moving to the interior, I am using a ¼in bowl gouge again to reduce the work to even proportions. The ⅜in or a spindle gouge would also do exactly the same work. I do not believe in slavishly adhering to a tool just because it is called a Bowl Gouge.

Fig. 10.17.   When the shape is roughed to within a little of the desired style, a freshly honed spindle gouge is the tool *I* use for the few final cuts. It is all a matter of what suits the individual turner, and what timber is being worked in the light of experience. It would be easy to say 'I have never found a timber I cannot work with a cutting tool', but I have not worked *all* timbers, so it is impossible to be pedantic.

Fig. 10.18.   However, a heavy scraper, very sharp, and maintained in this condition will serve very well. With the availability today of the scrapers with HSS (high speed steel) or even tungsten inserts, a far greater spectrum of work can be completed with these tools, and with the absence of endgrain, consideration should be given to this method.

Fig. 10.19.   A few fine finishing cuts to the outside of the bowl and the project is ready for finishing.

Fig. 10.20.   As the drawing indicates, the time taken to calculate the size of the individual rings in the proposed lamination for a given design will be well rewarded in the saving of material. Conversely, as it is my practice to make a lot of blanks at one time, this method lends itself to the reverse procedure. If a number of blanks all the same size and lay-up are produced, templates of intended styles can be placed over a drawing to ascertain if the given lamination will comply. The template can then be used in working to ensure not only the style but that there is enough material remaining at all times to work with safety. I would not want to be specific with regard to how fine/thin such work should be completed. This will depend on such factors as the timber used, overall size of the project, even shape and certainly experience. As a guide, for this size 12in × 4in, not much less than ⅜in or ¼in at most, should be contemplated until experience is gained.

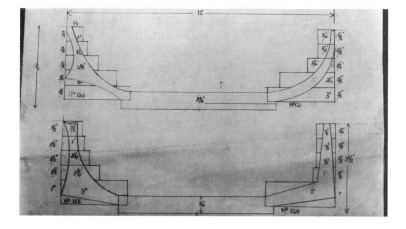

Ring segment turning for bowl work

Fig. 11.1   The method we are about to discuss must be just about the most economic, or to use the modern jargon, 'cost effective' usage of timber possible. By using the four corners that would be the only waste, a plinth can be produced, and apart from a modicum of shavings and a little sawdust, the remainder of the material ends up in the finished product. That being said, one is very much confined to bowls, and I have been unable to find an alternative use for the method. We must not discount alternative decorative possibilities, however, and while I have produced the example in its simplest form, you can add your own ideas about using veneer in the joints, both vertical and horizontal, or pre-laminating any of the original boards from which the assembly is cut. The thickness of veneer will make little difference to the true circle on assembly, but beware of any insert that will induce any form of ellipse; the problem is at once overcome by including any of the aforesaid in the original lamination. Any or all of these methods will produce, in some combination, most dramatic effects.

Fig. 11.2.   While the configuration of this style may appear to be unstable, this figure is an indication of the stability. It is without a plinth.

Fig. 11.3.   From four boards of 1in × 4in, stuff glued in pairs, with no adhesive in the centre line but held in place with cramps, a centre is established in the usual way. A piece of protective covering is secured with self-adhesive double sided tape to enable the circles to be scribed.

Fig. 11.4.　As the material we are working on in this instance is *net*, the point of the compass would mark the work and this is best avoided. The circles here, to provide a finished bowl of 5in high by 12in diameter, are set 1in apart.

Fig. 11.5.　While it would be difficult to mix the components after sawing, it is a wise precaution to number or letter them, and certainly necessary if making more than one at a time. I find this type of work pays dividends if one makes several blanks while the machine angles are set up, even if I don't work them or need them at once.

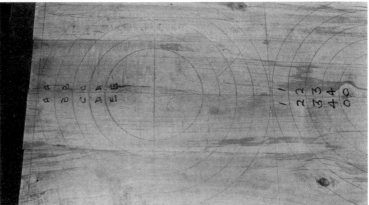

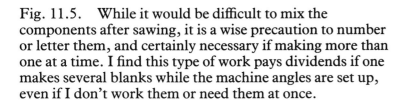

Fig. 11.6.　When the sawing sections are scribed and identified it will be necessary to square the centreline completely round the piece that will become the base of the assembly, in order to present a centre for mounting. It will be obvious that there is not a great deal of thickness in the assembled blank, so meticulous marking out will be necessary, as will careful sawing of the rings.

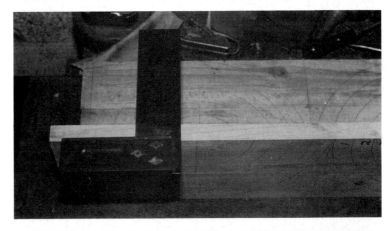

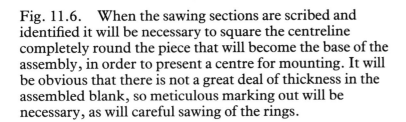

Fig. 11.7.　It is optional how the first cut is made, either with the bandsaw table in its right-angle mode or, as will be required for the remainder, set at an angle of 45°. In this example I am demonstrating the former as this gives a little more timber at the rim of the blank for the purpose of styling. If the latter mode is employed, the blank will be a true 45° angle right through to the top. The outer ring is therefore cut first, and it would be prudent to spend a little time practising on some inexpensive stuff (if cutting with a bandsaw at an angle of 45° is not among your accomplishments).

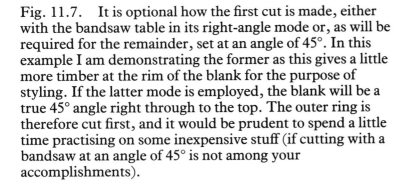

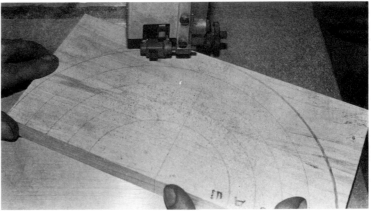

Fig. 11.8.   The small bandsaw is not the most precise tool in my experience, nor in fairness, is it intended to be. However, care should be taken to obtain a sawn angle of as near 45° as is possible; a degree of two out will make little difference. I find a protractor is excellent for the purpose of setting the angle.

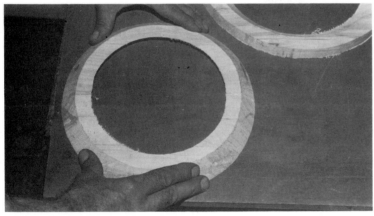

Fig. 11.9.   With the bandsaw table angled, the rings can be sawn. A turner's 'skip tooth' blade is recommended as its teeth have plenty of set, so provide clearance in the kerf and make for easier guiding. Take your time, there are no prizes for speed, and be mindful of your fingers.

Fig. 11.10.   In assembly, the rings are lightly glued and held together by hand for a few moments. Work must be done on a dead flat surface. As this joint is of minimal importance an impact adhesive will do. I prefer to use P.V.A., then, after holding together, slide them to one side while completing the others. Note the shape of cut form in the ring to the top right of this figure. This will be the top ring of the assembly.

Fig. 11.11.   With the adhesive set for a few hours at least, and preferably overnight, the glue squeeze on the mating surfaces can be *very* lightly sanded. Abrasive of no coarser grit than 320g should be used and no more than to remove the excess adhesive. Hold the work with a piece of clean paper or rag to avoid contamination of the mating surfaces. I have stressed this point on several occasions and some may think such care to be unnecessary. Try the following: take two pieces of, say, 1in × 2in a foot long, mark off the first two inches of each and press a sweaty hand on this area, on both pieces. Assemble with adhesive in the normal way, leave to cure, and you will, in all probability, be able to break the joint with little or no effort. The same experiment can be tried, crushing the joint in cramps or bench vice, and the effort will be very revealing.

Fig. 11.12. With the component assembled dry I have marked heavily in ink the joint in the rings. As long as these joints do not come together, there is no rule as to where they should be placed. To the right is another line from top to bottom to indicate where in assembling, once any format is selected. The advantage of keeping the saw table in the right angled position is indicated here; had the whole been cut at 45°, the shape would be identical from top to base.

Fig. 11.13. No specialised apparatus is required for assembly. A pair of steel rules is enough to ensure the rings are in the correct position immediately above each other. Tests on the four quadrants will be required, and if felt necessary, repeated after weighting.

Fig. 11.14. It is imperative to assemble on a dead flat surface. Take care to bring the weights down in such a way as to stop any of the rings sliding. A smooth and even distribution of adhesive will help to achieve this end. The blank must be left in this mode at least until the adhesive sets hard, and no attempt to work should be made until it is cured. Be patient, it will pay in the end, both from a safety point of view and for a perfectly finished product.

Fig. 11.15. It would be fair to suggest this is the ultimate in lazy turning, as only the minimum of work is required and possible. The style is restricted to very little more than cleaning up the original shape. I have found it best to commence with the rim and to work the bowl to a finish completely as I proceed to the base. It is as well to take great care as the base is reached, in order that it is not marked with the gouge. It is a difficult area to clean up.

Fig. 11.16. The blank as seen here is mounted on a simple screw chuck, or small faceplate. Either a bowl gouge or, as I prefer, a spindle gouge, will quickly clean up the blank, which should finish approx ½in thick, perhaps a little less as the stuff dictates. Despite the optically confusing configuration of this build-up, the blank will commence working at a thickness of 1in, and the only differential will be how accurately the rings were built into the turning blank.

Fig. 11.17. While this format looks unstable, it is surprisingly steady, even when loaded with fruit in an unbalanced position. However, if a plinth is required it is a simple matter to provide one from the four corners removed in Fig. 11.7. One could add inserts of some sort in the joints, face top and/or bottom or whatever. The shooting board is invaluable here, and again, when building up, the components should be matched carefully and marked, both for identification in working in assembly, and if felt necessary, for grain direction.

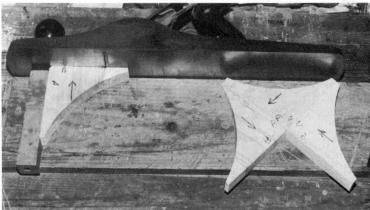

Turning exotic timbers

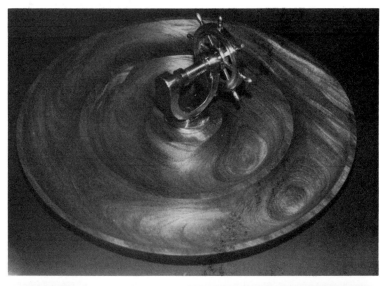

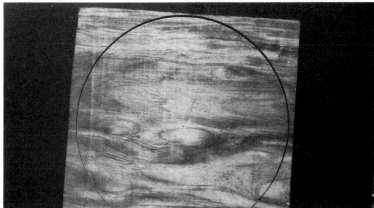

Fig. 12.1.   From time to time we come across a piece of exquisite stuff, perhaps even in a size that is just what we want for a specific project. I have a habit of putting such pieces away, thinking 'I will work that one day', but secretly being afraid to do so in case I spoil a unique piece that will possibly never be seen again. The fear stems from the fact that, being a new timber, I have no knowledge of its workability, its quirks, what it likes in way of tooling etc. Is it dry? Will it move much after working? What finish will be in order? So, after getting this piece of New Guinea Rosewood out a few times, admiring it, then putting it away again, I thought it time I made the effort to produce the nut cracker bowl that suited its size. As will be obvious from the finished photograph, the work went according to plan, so although there is no cliff-hanger for the reader, it was not quite the same for the turner. The brass mechanisms are available from various firms who cater for turners. The timber is a deep golden brown with light gold highlights, 15in in diameter and 1½in deep.

Fig. 12.2.   A few strokes of a hand plane over the sawn surface to reveal the delight beneath, and to give the very first indication of workability. Cross marked, a circle scribed, and the disc sawn to be ready for mounting. The sawing is also an indication of 'things to come', and was no problem. My confidence increased; perhaps I'm not such a coward after all.

Fig. 12.3.   Even the smallest of my faceplates would have left screwholes outside the periphery of the mechanism I was about to use. Always check these little things. However, by now I had some idea of the density of this timber, so I felt a single screwchuck would suffice for the preparation of the rear or base. This screwchuck was fitted to what would ultimately be the top or inside of the project.

Fig. 12.4.   After rounding with a gouge, the base was smoothed to a finish with an extra carefully prepared scraper. Perfectly flat for this platter, as it will contain either nuts or fruit, and to work a plinth would make it unstable. I now knew both tools would work with no excitement, at least in this convex configuration.

Fig. 12.5.   The timber was light enough to be suitable for this project, but was obviously strong enough to take a 2in collet. A large diameter would be fine, but there is a delicacy about 'small' that I like. The recess for the expanding collet was produced with a skew chisel, and with the same tool a recess to accept the head of the bolt that will retain the mechanism was worked. A relatively new product on the market is a range of sanding discs produced specifically for the turner, available in a number of sizes from 1in diameter upwards, some with self-adhesive pads, and now I understand, with 'Velcro'. The pads are of about ½in thick soft sponge rubber to follow the contours of a turning, and the sanding discs range in grit from fine to coarse. In my opinion, this product has revolutionised sanding for the turner, and is used with the lathe running at approx 1500rpm.

Fig. 12.6.   Fit into a drill of reasonable power, 600 watts or so. Or if using a lighter product, use with care and rest periodically so as not to overload the motor. At a normal drill speed, of about 3000rpm, just stroke the surface to be finished in either direction, i.e. from the centre out or vice versa. It is quite astonishing how quickly a reasonably tooled surface can be finished with this tool, and, due to the action, sanding rings, however fine, that would be left with normal sanding, will be completely eliminated. The process of going up in grit of abrasive still applies of course.

Fig. 12.7.   The next 'experiment' was what finish to use. I require a hard one for the outside, and a non gloss for the inside. Thus Danish oil was selected, and tried on one of the sawn off corners to see if it did anything I didn't like. It was perfect. It is always as well to test a finish on a spare piece of the same stuff, as various products, that will serve on some timbers, can be unsuitable for others. Note the slight darkening effect here where the Danish oil is applied.

Fig. 12.8.   With the remainder oiled with a priming coat, to protect from finger marking and to seal, the further coats will be applied after complete finishing and the work finally replaced in the lathe for buffing to a shine, on the outside only. For articles like this, which will contain anything of a rough or abrasive nature, a shine looks delightful when new but is soon scuffed and appears unsightly. The chuck is fitted while in this position and checked for true running.

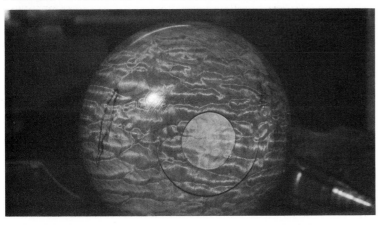

Fig. 12.9.   Always check the effect various finishes will have on a given piece of stuff. This was a piece of Quilted Maple, a timber I had no experience of. The sender described it as 'one of the finest examples I have ever seen'; perhaps the reader will join me in my complete agreement with the statement! Pale cream in colour, with a grain that I have no need to describe, but delivered cut in disc form, thus no corners to experiment with. The remedy was simple, clean up the area required for initial mounting i.e. that part that was to become the inside and try a few experiments. This example has been treated with Danish oil, and for me this was unacceptable. It changed the natural cream colouring to dark brown, and to my mind this treatment bastardises the true and natural beauty of the timber.

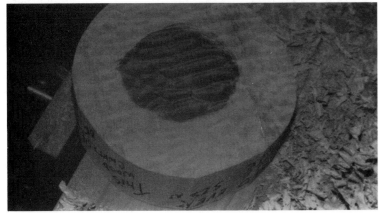

Fig. 12.10.   With the outside of the bowl worked to a finish I had established that a clear lacquer would make little difference to the colour of the stuff, other than the effect seen here. The bowl has been given a sealing coat but the centre remains as worked. The colour change is minimal.

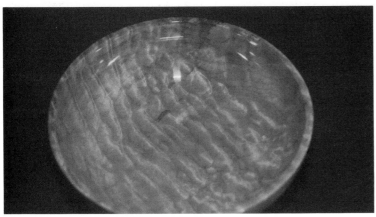

Fig. 12.11.   The finished piece. It was a pity the stuff arrived in disc form. As it was I had few options in using it; a bowl was the only choice. Had the square been available I could have produced several pieces from its original size of 9in × 3in. It is worth keeping this in mind when cutting up stuff to store or dry.

Fig. 12.12.   Using a 'Superflute', one of the HSS bowl gouges we hear so much about, the two hollows were quickly worked, and finished. The outside hollow worked at 1000rpm and the inner hollow at 1500rpm. Peripheral speed should be taken into consideration on a diameter such as this. It was interesting to find that turning was identical in finish on the two hollows at two different speeds.

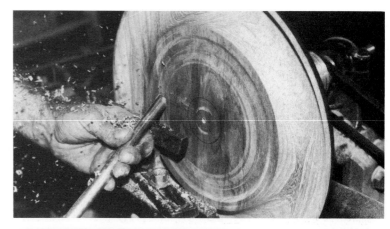

Fig. 12.13.   A recess was again required to take a small boss on the base of the mechanism, and at the same time, the hole for the bolt shank worked. I have a very narrow skew, ⅛in wide, which is ideal for this operation, and in this mode of turning preferable to using a drill.

Fig. 12.14.   Testing not only for fit but effect, I leave a timber surround to the base of the mechanism. I feel this is aesthetically more acceptable than working to the size of the brass base, which being 'fettled' castings are seldom completely circular anyway.

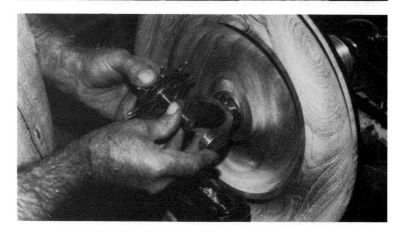

Fig. 12.15.   Dark Teak oil was chosen for the face of the project. It seals well, protects if given two or three applications, and is suitable for easy maintenance in the home. I had again tested this with an application to another corner and found, while it darkened more than I liked when first applied, it was much lighter when dry.

Fig. 12.16.   Let us look at a couple of much more common timbers, and formats. From left to right a piece of burr (burl in America) Elm, with an added bonus of that change of colour in grain. Then two pieces of Chestnut burr, the centre piece looking a little like a loaf of bread, and the one to the right worked to show exactly what is inside the 'loaf'. Sawyers will discard such pieces and relegate them to the firewood box, which gives the turner a chance to pick up some very inexpensive and exquisite timber. We will 'process' the one on the right in a moment.

Fig. 12.17.   Another pet hate of the sawyer is timber he finds to be 'spalted' or 'dozywood' (the first is the American term, the second English). It is diseased, perhaps because of bad storage – letting it lie on the earth too long before conversion, or stacking planks without sticks or with sticks that are too thin. The disease is occasioned by excessive and permanent damp, and is at once checked when the timber is properly dried. It is nevertheless a *rot* and this fact should not be overlooked. If a careful check is made for the soft spots these can be discarded. If a watchful eye is kept in working, soft spots unseen to start with can appear. Some beautiful timber can be obtained, and sometimes for free. The disease is *not* contagious.

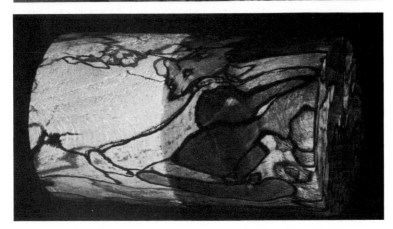

Fig. 12.18.   The piece displayed in the previous figure is seen here. About two thirds of the square was salvaged and turned to a cylinder. Half is sealed with one application of Danish oil to indicate again the effect or change of colour. I think it would be fair to say that Beech, while having its use, is not the most exciting timber in the world. This is a piece of 'dozy' Beech, and I would suggest delightful at that. We will see it again later on in Chapter 16.

Fig. 12.19.   Those in the habit of working 'tailor made' timber would be entitled to some apprehension. Let's see if I can change their minds. Securely attach it to a faceplate and thoroughly check to ensure all the parts of the lathe are secure (toolrest, holder, etc). Make a few turns to double check, and set the speed to not faster than 1000rpm.

Fig. 12.20.   I use a ⅜in spindle gouge, honed to a razor edge. Take a few light cuts for a few revolutions, just enough to have a look at what is going on under that rough exterior. This will also bring the uneven stuff to a more balanced form, then the lathe speed can be increased if required.

Fig. 12.21.   Now comes the time to decide what to do with such a piece. A bowl perhaps, perfect for a base for table lamp or similar purpose. Sometimes I even put such pieces away until inspiration strikes. I have a large stock of such pieces!

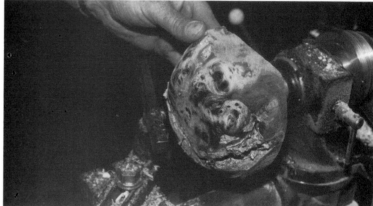

Fig. 12.22.   I decided to continue working until most of the imperfections were removed, and to produce a handled candle holder. Here we see that rather 'uncouth' piece of stuff take on a more refined appearance. 'Beneath that rough exterior lies a heart of gold'.

Fig. 12.23.   Further turning would have removed this last part of the unevenness of the blank, but to continue would have reduced the overall size. I wanted to avoid this, so a cove was worked to remove the worst of the affected area.

Fig. 12.24.   As the project was to be a candle holder the base needs to be stable, so no more than was necessary was taken from this area. We have discussed filling and repairs in general; the working was left at this stage.

Fig. 12.25.   The bulk of the waste to accommodate the candle and the glass funnel was removed with a narrow gouge, ¼in will do. If the funnel used does not have little lugs at its base, to permit airflow, two or three small holes can be drilled at the base of the worked housing in the timber. About ¼in diameter will usually be sufficient, just enough to allow air to enter the funnel or the candle will go out after burning for a few moments.

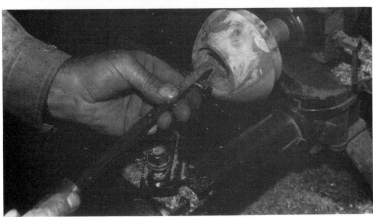

Fig. 12.26.   As straight sided holes are required for the two components, a few light cuts made with the long corner of the skew will tidy it up a treat.

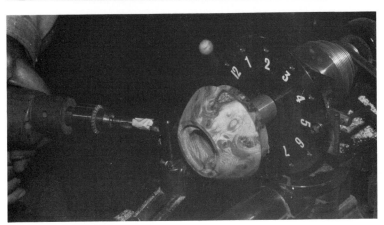

Fig. 12.27.   As in Chapter 5, a hole is produced to accept the handle. I find a jig of some sort invaluable for this work, and while the dividing disc is not required to work any repetition here, it serves to trap the work. My lathe does not have any other means of doing so.

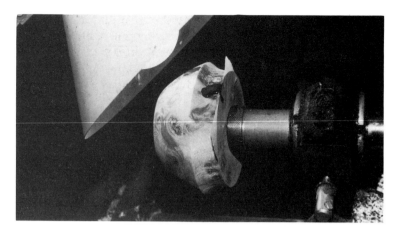

Fig. 12.28.   I use epoxy almost exclusively to effect filling of this nature, see Chapter 5 for details. By bringing the lamp to the position shown here, gentle heat for a few moments will make the thick epoxy somewhat more liquid. This will allow it to run into the cracks or imperfections. Always overfill for best results, the epoxy can then be worked with sharp tools.

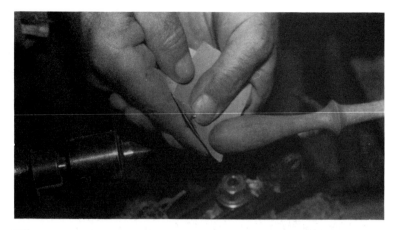

Fig. 12.29.   The handle is turned, sanded and polished, this one with friction polish. Matted with 0000 steel wool used with furniture polish, this will be compatible in finish to the base.

Fig. 12.30.   The finished base after two applications of teak oil, dried for a couple of days, and then replaced in the lathe for burnishing. A cork base which will not *slip* was applied and a most attractive product quickly resulted. Some would perhaps say the rather plain area of this piece (seen in the working photograph, Fig. 12.25) would detract from the heavily burred area. For this reason, I placed the handle there. I would suggest that the area actually adds interest to the piece due to its total difference. The timber is, of course, Chestnut, quite common, and shows that a visit to a sawmill on occasions, with a few pounds in the pocket and an empty car will pay for the journey.

Fig. 12.31.   The finished candle holder.

Fig. 12.32. Some comments on knots. So often it is suggested, 'take a piece of stuff, perfect and knot free'. Such an attitude makes a great deal of timber redundant, though it is well meant with regard to safety in working. I feel it should not be taken literally, as long as the stuff will not be liable to fracture due to a knot. If one falls out while working, glue it back again. To make the point, here, we have a nutmeg grinder produced from a piece of stuff the nature of which is 90% knot. It is a section of Cypress Pine pictured back in the place from whence it came. The rest of the timber in the billet is, to say the least, bland by comparison.

Fig. 12.33. Thuya Burr, a North African timber, which is very rarely seen in the solid. It is used almost exclusively for the production of veneers. A good friend found some in his travels and made me a present of this piece. I would say one of the most delightful timbers I have ever worked: extremely oily, much more so than Teak, with an exquisite perfume, quite easy to work though a little care was required in the cross grain on the stem. Made completely on the Coronet Mini expanding collet and seen here supported by the tailstock for final polishing.

Fig. 12.34. Another gift, this time from America, Big Leaf Maple. I am still not sure which way round I worked this timber; it may have been with the grain across the lathe or in line. It doesn't matter now it is finished. Completed on the Coronet Mini expanding collet chuck, and finished with friction polish.

Fig. 12.35. A nutcracker bowl in Ebony, from a timber configuration similar to that discussed in Figs. 2.36 to 2.38. The delightful grain in the cream sapwood makes a swirling exit into the black of the base of the anvil. The tiny black dots add to the charm of the piece. This piece was turned to permit the sapwood to break out in the rim in one place. With mallet faces in Lignum Vitae, as is the slightly raised face of the anvil. The handle of the mallet is Blackwood, with just a hint of sap attached. It is designed so that the handle rests on the anvil, making the whole an attractive mix of similar-looking timbers from India (Ebony), Africa (Blackwood), and the West Indies (Lignum, perfect for the purpose, and blending delightfully).

Fig. 12.36. Another exquisite timber from America, Mesquite. This is the red species; there is also a brown one. The interlocking grain shows translucent highlights after finishing. Produced here (in another style I like very much) with a deeply undercut rim. This is very much a job for a 'right handed' half round scraper in my experience. For outboard turning, the reverse would apply.

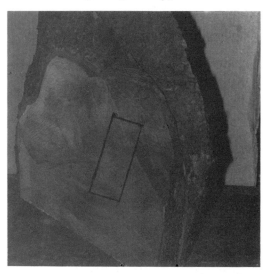

Fig. 12.37. Another example of how the turner can make delightful use of 'rejected' timbers. We have the ends of two boards, cut rift from the log, and discarded by a cabinet maker. I can demonstrate again where beautiful timber comes from. The boards were 3in stuff and I have placed the two back together as in natural growing form. The one at the front has the base of a limb showing, to me an area of great interest. The marked section was removed on the bandsaw (or as near to the marked section as I am able to reproduce here).

Fig. 12.38. Propped up on a spare piece of stuff is the goblet made from the piece and replaced in its original position. This timber was nothing more than Ash, usually straight grained and without great interest, but I would suggest this example indicates what can be found in timber, without great expense or difficulty.

Face and between-centres turning

Fig. 13.1. This project is taken from a sailing ship's lamp. Oil lamps had to maintain an upright stance, so the 'gimbal' was the answer. Whichever way the table or wall tilts, the lamp will always remain perpendicular. This project can be left in this tilting mode but I feel it is better to secure the fixing pins with adhesive and leave the rest to the observer's imagination. I have styled this one to use a wax candle, but it would be simple to electrify. The method is ideal for wall lighting, as we see in Fig. 13.3., and the wallplate is, of course, a split turning. Dressing table mirrors, photostands, pedestal ashtrays etc are all variations on this technique, and wall mounted plant pot holders are very attractive in this style. Made in Andaman Padauk, this one is an interesting and exacting article to produce. Here I have produced it in part solid and part lamination, but either could be used throughout.

Fig. 13.2. The same lamp used as a wall light fitting.

Fig. 13.3.   A variation on the same theme, but with only one ring. This model I leave free to move as it will do so only in one direction and it lends interest to the turning. The heavy base makes it automatically self righting, and the cable prevents too much movement.

Fig. 13.4.   Starting with the double laminated centre ring we have a single lay-up, endgrain to endgrain. This format has little or no strength, and must be worked, if necessary, as in Chapter 4. If 'Flexicramps' are not available, hoseclips will substitute and are obtainable in large sizes or can be coupled together. Here we have one ring assembled with a hoseclip and a further hoseclip added to positively locate a second ring that will be glued in 'brickwall' fashion, thus providing adequate strength for working.

Fig. 13.5.   Lightly cramp the two components together. This technique can be continued to increase the size of the blank if required.

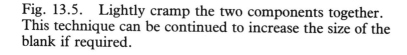

Fig. 13.6.   The 'horseshoe' is produced in the same way but here in triple lamin form. A centring disc will be required to work it, so it can serve also as a positive centre from which to assess any dimensions required. Any further measurements, as here, can be laid off using the joints in the lamination as a reference (as they must be accurate). Three holes will be required in this component, one to secure the base and two for the centre piece.

Fig. 13.7.   It is of the utmost importance to ensure that these holes are both equidistant on the three points and perfectly square with the sides. A drillpress will be a great asset, or the lathe itself can be used to achieve this. I have inked in the joint here to indicate the use of this in predetermining the position. It is preferable to make the holes before turning, thus any spelch produced in drilling will be removed in working.

Fig. 13.8.   With the o.d. rough sawn and set up in the 'Boulter' with the centring disc removed, the inside can be worked to the required dimensions and checked for squareness. Alternatively, a moulding can be worked either now, or later as we will see. An area of about ¼in dead centre should be left square with the jig for subsequent mounting and working.

Fig. 13.9.   The disc of ply is mounted on a screwchuck fitted with a setscrew and turned to a snug fit to the i.d. of the workpiece, or, if a moulding has been started, to the ¼in area suggested in Fig. 13.8. As we have holes in this component, we may as well make use of them, much as we will do in Fig. 17.21 with pins. This time we can use 'pegs' that are made on the lathe and will support larger and heavier work, see Fig. 13.14 for details. With the workpiece set up like this, it will be the same as working a solid piece. The snug fit to the disc coupled to the stability provided by the pegs will permit any styling required with no fear of striking anything metallic.

Fig. 13.10.   The outside can be worked either in the position of the previous figure, or with the work reversed. The setscrew method of mounting the disc offers this advantage which, if working solid stuff, could be useful if there are endgrain problems. The reverse face is, of course, easily accessible as well.

Fig. 13.11.   Sanding is possible all round. The centre, which cannot be sanded at this time, would have been completed while the work was in the 'Boulter'.

Fig. 13.12.   Again measurement is unnecessary, other than the actual opening size required, as the lamination will indicate the line to cut.

Fig. 13.13.   The rough sawn edges can be finished on the disc sander. If a proprietary unit is not available for your particular lathe, it is a simple matter to produce a home-made version. A disc is turned true on a faceplate of a size to accommodate sanding discs, and the discs are attached with 'Flexstic' or similar, *not* with impact adhesive. A table can be produced and fitted to the toolrest holder of the lathe.

Fig. 13.14.   The centre ring ready to complete in the same way as the horseshoe. The pegs detailed are a simple between-centres turning; they can be used almost indefinitely for this technique. In producing the *four* holes in this component, remember only *two* will be required right through. The two to locate the horseshoe will be stopped for neatness.

Fig. 13.15.   The lamp or candle holder is 'X' marked. Using the centre thus provided, a line for the pivoting pin holes is accurately produced.

Fig. 13.16.   We have discussed how accurate drilling can be performed in the lathe itself. However, if this facility is not available, a drillpress or even careful hand drilling will be the alternatives. It is most important that the two holes are in the same plane, as the centres for turning, and the stuff should be mounted between centres with this in mind.

Fig. 13.17.   Most chimneys will, or should be, produced with lugs in the moulding at the base of the glass to permit airflow. If such a provision is not available, drill four holes in the same plane as in the next figure in the rebate for the chimney, say, ⅛in diameter larger than the width of the rebate. This will provide adequate ventilation for bulb or candle. These holes will not need to go right through, so will be virtually invisible but bridge the thickness of the glass. The rebate for the chimney needs to be a slack fit to allow for movement of the glass when heated.

Fig. 13.18. A hole for the dowel of the candle holder can be worked or, if an electrical fitting is intended, the correct diameter drilled for the nipple. The flange type, that will accept the bayonet nipple Edison screw fitting, is preferable.

Fig. 13.19. A mandrel can be used when the work is reversed, or a longer screw than usual fitted to a screwchuck. This screw will locate in the indent left by the tip of the drill used in Fig. 13.18. Any further styling can now be completed.

Fig. 13.20. If it is intended to leave the finished piece in the form of a genuine gimbal, the base of this component must contain a counterweight. Lead is the best metal to use as its size-weight ratio will permit the heaviest weight in the smallest area.

Fig. 13.21. The holder for the candle is produced on the screwchuck. It is also possible to produce a 'drip tube' to cover the electrical fitting in this way, or, as a progression of Fig. 5.12. Such a drip tube can be left in polished timber form, or the rim dipped in adhesive, thickened with fine sawdust, then inverted to produce a 'candledrip' effect, and painted with a white radiator paint, which is both flexible and heat resistant.

Fig. 13.22. An ornamental finial for the base, to produce either a decorative effect or to contain the lead 'pig', is worked. This can be done in any of the ways we have so far discussed.

Fig. 13.23. The pivot pins are a simple screwchuck procedure, and a slight chamfer before parting off will permit ease of entry when the project is assembled.

Designing grinders

With all the electrical gadgetry available today, the old fashioned coffee grinder could be described as obsolete. However, judging by the number I am asked for and the range of mechanisms that are available for turners, this would seem not to be the case. Used as a form of kitchen *objet d'art*, as I understand most of these are, the one to the left of the picture is perhaps the most dramatic. It is also the most simple to fit, so we'll have a go at that one first. A little 'quirk' of mine is that I love to work with logs. I know we are told that to use timber with any heartwood in will end in disaster, but, as we will see when finished the one pictured in the centre doesn't have any heart left in anyway!

Fig. 14.1.   From left to right we have Cocobolo, English Oak, Indian Rosewood (staved base), with Indian Ebony collar. Again from left to right, the mechanisms are matt black, chromium silver, then brass, and in each I have replaced the handle with the same timber as the rest of the piece. Most of this type of work is used for purely decorative effect, but nevertheless all these styles will grind coffee in the event of a power cut.

Fig. 14.2.   A 'slab' is the name sawyers give to the first cut taken from a log. It is a format I like to make full use of. In some instances, such as bowl making, the most dramatic effects or balance of timber can be achieved. One side of the slab will be flat, so it is cross marked and a faceplate attached. I am using a single screw screwchuck with a screw projection of approx 1¼in (No 14 for the Coronet machines).

Fig. 14.3.   It is very difficult, or impossible, to mark a circle accurately on the area first to be worked. I mount on the lathe as described, fit a temporary stop to the toolrest, and by turning the work *by hand*, using any tool with a point, following the natural shape of the workpiece.

Fig. 14.4.   By removing the screwchuck it is then possible to take the work to the bandsaw with an accurately marked periphery and produce a disc ready to be returned to the lathe in more or less conventional form.

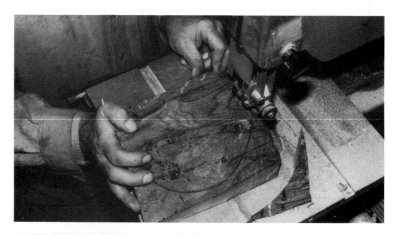

Fig. 14.5.   Returned to the lathe at the slowest speed (approx 500rpm). Ensure everything is well tightened, and test for clearance, which is essential when working irregular shapes. The rough and unbalanced form will soon be worked to a true shape. While roughing down work of this nature some vibration will possibly be experienced, and while I have not taken space in the introduction to stress the need for the lathe to be installed correctly, it will be obvious that a firm fixing for any machine tool is a must. I feel it is the responsibility of the manufacturer to provide comprehensive installation instructions for any particular machine.

Fig. 14.6.   I use a spindle gouge for this work and this tool is used to prepare a flat on (what will be) the top of the base piece.

Fig. 14.7.   Satisfied with the outside shape and finish, and following the normal procedure for bowl work, a fixing rebate for the chuck is worked. The only difference is that the same care and attention to the base of this rebate is not necessary, as it will be removed later. The chuck is the old pattern 6-in-1, fitted with expanding collet.

Fig. 14.8.   Simple bowl work is all that is required to hollow out the inside. I am taking a few final finishing cuts leaving plenty of thickness to the wall, to stop the finished product, with a large and heavy wheel, becoming top heavy. Combined with the diameter of the base there will be no fear of unsteadiness. When considering any design, functional or practical aspects should be examined in tandem with aesthetic appearance.

Fig. 14.9.   A rebate to accept the baseplate is produced using a 1/s ¼in skew chisel to a depth just slightly thicker than the baseplate. This will permit any cleaning up that may be required in the final finishing, e.g. removing glue squeeze.

Fig. 14.10.   A baseplate is fitted, and the adhesive allowed to cure. I had found a few scraps of plywood with a soft plastic finish and thought it would be ideal for this purpose. It did, however, show the screw holes and there was no way to cover them.

Fig. 14.11.   The base finished and polished after the hole, that will accept the ground coffee and provide the collar with a fitting, is worked. As a point of interest a friend used this method for the base of a most attractive 'anglepoise' lamp made in Ebony. He filled the hollow with scraps of lead collected from wheel weights etc. It goes to prove there is a use for everything. We must now produce the collar/bung.

Fig. 14.12.   A piece of matching, or contrasting, stuff is mounted on a single screwchuck and the periphery worked true to almost finished size. The required hole diameter is then produced about half way through, using the 1/s ¼in skew chisel. If a longish screw is in the chuck, avoid hitting it in working by leaving a small pip in the centre.

Fig. 14.13.   Always check carefully with vernier or calipers as the work proceeds.

Fig. 14.14. The spigot that will enter the base must be accurately worked, and be neither sloppy nor too tight. In practice I find that the base usually moves slightly and the hole becomes an ellipse. If the collar follows the same pattern, which it is likely to do, and if a good fit is produced, a slight twist when the two parts are united will render a 'locking' effect. A ⅜in beading/parting tool is being used to produce the spigot.

Fig. 14.15. Further styling can be completed, and the whole section sanded and polished. The fibreboard disc between the chuck and the work will protect the tool when the parting tool is inserted between it and the workpiece to a depth of ⁵⁄₁₆in or so. It's not critical, but must be deeper than the diameter of the hole worked in the next figure.

Fig. 14.16. Bring the toolrest to the front of the work and with a few light cuts join the parting cut, using the ¼in skew chisel. The finished workpiece will be severed cleanly, with a reasonably well finished inside. The inside can be cleaned up by hand if necessary, or placed in a form of the chuck used in Chapter 5 for finishing or even working. In practice, though, none of these suggestions should be necessary and the work will not be seen anyway. The mechanism can now be attached to the collar with small bolts, Japaned screws, or epoxy adhesive.

Fig. 14.17. The handles provided with the mechanisms can sometimes be of 'casual' manufacture, and 'dismal' material. I drive the pin holding the handle in position out, and replace the handle with one of my own make. Some of these mechanisms are made in cast iron so do take great care. Others are plastic or a form of aluminium.

Fig. 14.18. As the mechanisms vary, I will not suggest a standard way of working. However, the principle is very much the same with all. Someone fitted the handle in the first place, all we have to do is remove it in reverse order. Here we have a typical pin – the turned spigot that fits the handle can be seen. The old handle can be used to take the necessary dimensions for fitting the replacement.

Fig. 14.19. The Cocobolo used for the base and collar is a delightful timber in its own right, but here we have a small piece of quite exceptional beauty and indeed rarity. I have worked a lot of Cocobolo in my time, but this is the first time I have ever seen a piece like this. It is mounted on a screwchuck and supported with a revolving centre for working.

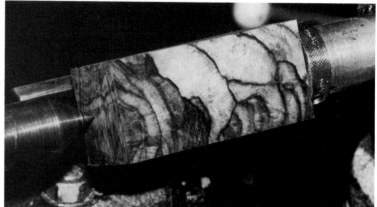

Fig. 14.20. With the grain running in all directions very sharp tools are required, and they must be maintained so. A final cut with a tool that has 'gone off' will, in all probability, spoil a treasured piece of stuff.

Fig. 14.21. The basic dimensions can be taken from the original. The depth prong of the vernier is invaluable for this part.

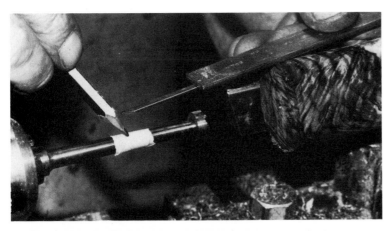

Fig. 14.22. The dimensions are transferred to a sawtooth bit fitted to the tailstock. I find the use of a piece of white tape on the bit, marked with a pencil for depth, is all the precision required.

Fig. 14.23. A hole of ⁵⁄₁₆in diameter is required to take the pin and allow free movement. Added to this a hole of a diameter to accept the washer, here ½in diameter, is necessary. Moreover, to avoid a sloppy fit the length of the ⁵⁄₁₆in hole must be accurate, i.e. it must match the distance between the shoulder of the spigot and the washer, plus just a touch to permit free movement. Drill only enough to avoid fouling the screw in the chuck; the hole can be completed when the work is removed from the lathe.

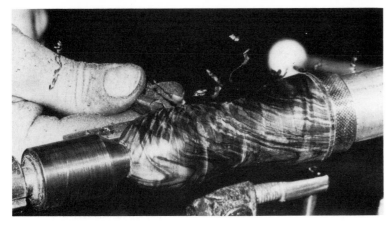

Fig. 14.24. With all the dimensional work completed, the handle can be styled with the work supported by the tailstock. When it's finished, polished and unscrewed, the ⁵⁄₁₆in diameter hole can be completed by hand.

Fig. 14.25. Fitted back in, the pin is peined with a hammer, and if it has been necessary to do any grinding to remove it in the first place, a dab of matt black paint applied. For a really fine finish a pip (see Chapter 15) can be turned to cover the ½in diameter hole in the outer end.

Fig. 14.26. I guess it has something to do with my laziness, that I enjoy working logs. They are, of course, round in the first place. I dare say science will eventually devise a way of growing trees square, and doubtless this will be to the delight of the sawyers. This was a piece I had waxed and weighed some time previously, see Chapter 5. The weight had stabilised, so the stuff was ready for working.

Fig. 14.27. It is not really difficult to find centre, even just by eye, and the stuff is mounted after preliminary turning on a screwchuck, with a 2in centre screw plus a further 1½in either side to render a good fixing in the *endgrain*. The whole is worked to a cylinder with a roughing out gouge.

Fig. 14.28. Some of the centre is removed to a depth that is comfortable for working, and a rebate is completed to accept the basepiece. The endgrain fixing is not the best or firmest so light cuts are required.

Fig. 14.29. Using the Coronet expanding collet chuck, or as here, a screwchuck, a base piece is prepared to fit the work which is then glued in position, if necessary using the lathe as a cramp. Note, this basepiece is 'capover'.

Fig. 14.30. As we now have access to the other end of the workpiece, the hollowing of the remainder can be completed, this time with more confidence as the fixing is more secure. At the same time the lid is formed in the same way as in Figs. 3.20 to 3.22.

Fig. 14.31. The lid is now *in situ* and the mechanism can be partly taken apart to provide the means of centring it while the epoxy adhesive used to fix it to the timber body of the grinder cures. Again, use the lathe as a cramp to permit overnight setting of the adhesive. The term setting is used throughout to indicate the adhesive 'drying', at which time it will not with most products be at full strength. 'Curing' indicates that full bond strength has been achieved and this will vary with the product used.

Fig. 14.32. There are many advantages to the use of logs. To mention just one, the format makes available stuff of a size that is not always available in the square from the sawyers. These two lamps are about 6in diameter and 15in high; the one to the left is Yew, the other Cypress Pine. I include this example to indicate not only what is possible but to lay emphasis on the need to look after timber. The Yew log was received by me freshly felled and I gave it the treatment I have described, so its degradation by the time it was dry enough to work was minimal. The Cypress log had been stored badly and some considerable filling was required in the finishing. Moreover, both pieces sported the expected knots, which add not only to the value of the finished pieces, but also to the challenge of working them. Each finished piece will have a balanced appearance as it will be in its perfectly natural state, merely shaped or styled by the woodturner.

Laminated work using rubber joints

Fig. 15.1. The making of lidded containers or bowls both in the solid and laminated is one of the favourites of most turners, and some delightful pieces can be produced. With economy and conservation of this precious material in mind, I felt that I should include another form of build-up, to which there is no limit to size, and which can be produced with ease without power tools, save the lathe. As long as each ring is produced from the same thickness stuff, there is no limit to the size of stuff used. But it must be of the same width, and the segments of the same size in length. With the addition of veneer between the rings or insertion of thin prepared banding (see Figures 16.18 to 16.22) at the joint of the rings when turning, the combinations are many and varied. The lay-up is also most useful for other projects, as we will see.

Fig. 15.2. I am using a mitre jig of professional make, but a home-made version will serve just as well. The finished segments for this configuration must be a true mitre of 45°.

Fig. 15.3. The stuff used must be square edged and it is best to shoot the sawcuts using a jig such as the one shown here, or as suggested before complete all the segments at one end first then move the jig for completion. This way, all the segments will be identical in length, and they *must* be so.

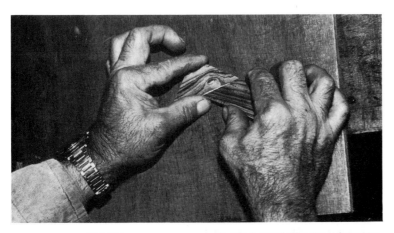

Fig. 15.4.   The endgrain of one is glued to the sidegrain of the next. Work on a dead flat surface, in a warm atmosphere. Hold the segments by hand for a few moments then *slide*, do not pick up, to continue the same process on the remainder. It will depend on the adhesive used but with most makes of P.V.A. the joint will accept very light handling after about ten minutes.

Fig. 15.5.   The secret of success in this work is to ensure that all the stuff is of uniform width, with edges square to the face, and perhaps most important that the 'rubbed' joint is dead level (as shown here). Any slight deviation at this point, either over or under, will make the final jointing of the complete ring a poor fit.

Fig. 15.6.   A sheet of some sort of fireproof material suspended over the workshop stove will set the adhesive off quite quickly, and render the pairs to be handled. Great heat is neither required nor desirable.

Fig. 15.7.   The pairs are then made up into fours, following the comments made previously. There is no strain placed on the original pair joint when making up the fours, which are now half of the complete circle. When making up the complete ring some strain on the previously made joints is inevitable so I leave the fours at least overnight before proceeding.

Fig. 15.8.   The two halves of four segments can now be brought together to form one complete ring. Leave again for at least overnight drying.

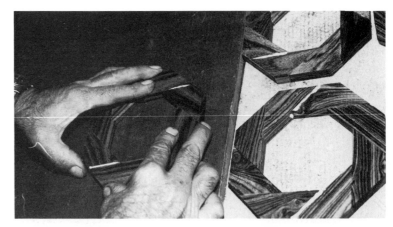

Fig. 15.9.   The ring can now be trimmed of glue squeeze with a plane. Beware of wax contamination, handling etc.

Fig. 15.10.   One complete ring. If the ring in the lathe is rotated *anticlockwise*, a tool presented to the left of the ring would cut with the grain and therefore, in effect, the 'right' way. Conversely if the ring be revolved *clockwise*, as it would be for outboard turning, the tool would be presented *against* the grain. While this may be a consideration in building up the blank for turning with sharp tools it would make little difference. In fact, some dramatic effects can be achieved with grain opposing. If the configuration has to be even, it will be a simple matter to mark the rings in readinesss for assembly into a blank.

Fig. 15.11.   Five rings ready to prepare the Flexicramp to size. The Flexicramp is to stop the rings sliding about when they are cramped together. The lay-up here is uniform, and for the first few this is the way to do it. When the technique is mastered, some interesting effects can be obtained by assembling out of uniformity, i.e. in a spiral pattern of joints, making sure the joints stagger from one ring to the next. In practice, it would be difficult to do otherwise. Using this method, measurement will be necessary to ensure the 'irregularity' is 'regular' in each layer. If it's random the same balance is not achieved.

Fig. 15.12.   Adhesive is applied to each ring as it is placed in an 'easy' fitting Flexicramp, and spread evenly over the entire surface.

Fig. 15.13.   By using two ply discs, pressure can be applied to the assembly while the adhesive cures. It is possible to work the flange for the base after a few hours setting in a warm workshop, as little strain is imposed on the blank which is supported by the jig anyway. That being said I feel it is worth considering the amount of work that has gone into this blank thus far, so is it really worth risking failure just for the sake of not waiting overnight?

Fig. 15.14.   Using the 'Boulter' jig, the flange to accept the base is produced. A lot of the inside working can be completed at this stage. If you decide to work any of the inside, and this involves turning the toolrest to achieve this, do be careful of the ends of the grips. A rap on the knuckles from iron is painful.

Fig. 15.15.   Using a spindle gouge, a disc for the base is soon worked to size.

Fig. 15.16.   If it is found more convenient, a wide ⅜in beading tool will certainly work a flat surface square with the face, and produce a fine fit. I find with this tool it is best traversed across the face of the work, taking a very fine cut to complete the size.

Fig. 15.17.   Here is one way of ensuring a good fit, especially if the stuff is a little too thick for the job. Establish the fit on the first ¹⁄₁₆in or so of the outer face. If this is too tight or too loose, the necessary adjustments can be made, and when the fit is perfect the remainder of the area can be sized to the same dimension.

Fig. 15.18.   Some timbers yield very well to a scraping action and a very good finish can be made with this tool. Light cuts will always produce the best results. Work the thickness required ready for the final adhesion in the blank.

Fig. 15.19.   Always distribute the adhesive evenly over the area of rebate, and apply a thin coat to the base.

Fig. 15.20.   A few weights are always useful in the workshop. Never pass up the chance of any old lead that is lying about – discarded wheel weights, foil from bottles etc. Lead has a very low melting point and a few prepared tins are most useful.

Fig. 15.21.   The rough exterior will soon be subdued with a gouge, here a roughing out gouge, but a spindle would serve as well. Note the direction of the grain in the ring at the base; but no problems in turning!

Fig. 15.22.   With the base set into the blank the work assumes all the aspects of a normal turning in solid timber. All that is necessary now is to decide what style you wish to produce.

Fig. 15.23.   While a roughing gouge is a useful tool for making the blank smooth, I find a spindle gouge the tool to use for shaping a relatively small box such as this. The examples displayed are almost reversals of each other in design form, and the spindle gouge will follow the gentle curves with ease.

Fig. 15.24.   A piece of matching timber is mounted on a screwchuck so as to permit the inside to be shaped, clearing the waste away with a gouge and finishing with a domed scraper. A short screw is used in the chuck, but take care not to strike it in working if the lid is to be turned very thin.

Fig. 15.25.   The lid is sized to a really snug fit in the box, as it will be simple to ease the fit later in final finishing. The entire outside can be blended into the shape of the box if you wish. It is as well to support the work with the tailstock, but, if the design calls for its withdrawal to gain access to any particular part, so long as the lid is a tight (very snug) fit in the box it will be workable without slipping.

Fig. 15.26.   The whole job can now be sanded and finished as one piece and in this mode a hole can be produced in the same way as in Chapter 17 for the fitting of the knob.

Fig. 15.27. The inside can now be sanded and finished and the fit of the lid eased (to what I call a 'positive fit') with abrasive paper. It is worth mentioning here that to take a cut of say 1/64in from the working side i.e. to ease this lid with a tool, would be more than ample, and would render a very slightly 'sloppy' fit. However, a cut of 1/16in on the working side when turning would represent 1/8in removed *overall* and that would be a bit too much.

Fig. 15.28. Most lids will have the fixing screw hole present, even the dowel of the knob showing sometimes. There is a saying in most trades, 'If you can't hide it, *show* it to advantage'. A well made 'pip' can not only hide the blemish, but actually enhance the appearance of the inside of the work.

Fig. 15.29. To produce such a pip, a short length of stuff is mounted on a screwchuck, or similar, from which several can be produced at one time and stored for later use. Turned to a cylinder and the crown of the pip cut with either a skew chisel or, as here, a parting tool presented on its side.

Fig. 15.30. The shank is turned to the correct diameter, usually to fit the hole made by the screwchuck, either in the dowel of the knob if it is shown, or the hole used to work the lid.

Fig. 15.31. It is sanded and polished, then cut off with a chisel. The operation can be repeated as often as there is material left to work.

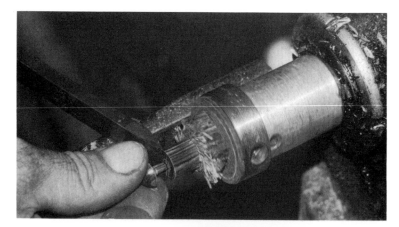

Fig. 15.32. By using a short screw, little waste will be caused and the few spare pips can be stored away for use in other projects.

Fig. 15.33. As with all laminating, the effects can be most interesting when a design is worked from a blank. For this reason it is worth stopping from time to time when shaping a project to study the formation of the exposed jointing and to see if a little cut here, or a bend in the design there, will enhance this, or prevent it from becoming unsightly. Here is an example: note the joints on the inside of the box, which is worked square with the base, are vertical, as would be expected. However on the outside of the same joint it takes on a sloping effect, added to which the ring at the top is vertical inside and outside. Considerable fun can be enjoyed 'explaining' to admirers how this 'ultra skilled craftsmanship' is effected!

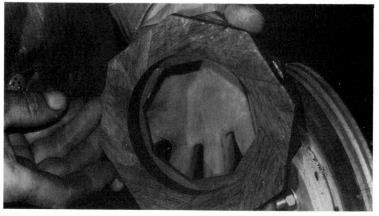

Fig. 15.34. These methods can be implemented from selected stuff, specially cut for the purpose, but can, of course, also be used on all sorts of odds and ends. As seen with the production of 'pips' nothing should ever be considered waste or scrap. I find, when setting about bevelling or shooting 'sessions' I prepare everything in sight and inevitably end up with far more than is actually required for an anticipated run of work. Odd rings, even odd segments as long as they conform in size, can be pressed into use. Pot stands, clocks, barometers, frames and so on can be produced from the leftovers. Here we have a couple of spare rings, set together and rebated in the jig.

Fig. 15.35. Great trees that may have taken decades to grow are felled in minutes, and by the factories used up almost as quickly. It is for this reason, and not because I am 'stingy' that I try to make the best use of this precious gift of nature. Even the centring discs can be used over and over again.

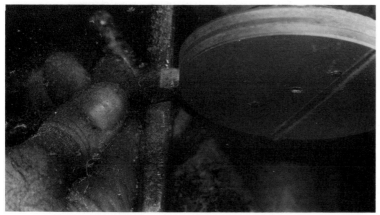

Fig. 15.36. From this odd ring we can produce a picture frame quite easily and quickly. On a faceplate a disc of ply is secured and turned to a snug fit to the rebate. For picture frames make the rebate about ⅜in deep. This will allow for the picture, the glass, and a good stiff backing.

Fig. 15.37. For the sort of project that will require fixing hanging points in use, two lugs are secured and the frame is held firmly, in the front by the rebate, and at the rear as seen. If the rear of the project will be visible in use the 'drive pin' method can be employed.

Fig. 15.38. The blank is now workable on the edge and the face, and is turned to the desired design to remove the rough edges.

Fig. 15.39. Bring the toolrest round to the front face and complete the centre opening. As the mounting disc is immediately behind, there will be no fear of spelch or of damage to the tool.

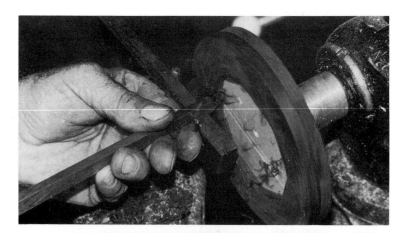

Fig. 15.40. The face of the work can then be completed. I am using a heavy domed scraper to finish the slightly hollow shape.

Fig. 15.41. The scraper is often shunned, indeed I may appear to do so at times. This is quite unintentional, as there are many uses for this tool and it has its rightful place in the turner's toolkit. Always use it as shown here – a good long handle tucked under the arm and presented thus will make for safe and positive cutting. It is not a 'hit or miss' tool and should always be kept very sharp.

Fig. 15.42. Finally, after sanding, polish with shavings. I prefer scraper shavings, as these will be fine and will have no hard lumps in them to score the finish, and I keep a bag for just this purpose. The finishing can now be applied, and if such product requires the turning to be returned to the lathe, for burnishing etc, the method will permit this.

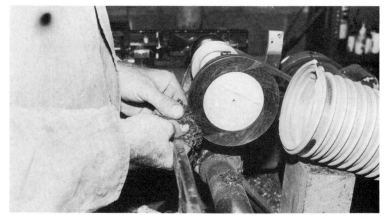

Fig. 15.43.   To lay emphasis on two factors, the use of odds and ends and the use of scrapers, we have here a few ends of Tulipwood (Dalbergia Frutescens). It is rare, hard to come by, and very expensive. These ends were *wider* than they were long so to get the best coverage from the available material I cut them for bevelling in the opposite way to those demonstrated in Fig. 4.3, i.e. to end up with a blank with grain running radially.

Fig. 15.44.   This means the cut is taken from the *endgrain*. It could be suggested that this is the weakness of the scraper – it won't satisfactorily work endgrain. Not so here, as it left a perfect finish indicated by the shaving thrown.

Fig. 15.45.   The front face was however a different story. The scraper did not like this at all and the final finish was produced with a gouge. It is for these reasons I feel it is unwise to be dogmatic about the use of tools for specific purposes. Differing timbers, applications, even turners, will all produce a variety of circumstances. I suggest you try the same and see how you get on. If it doesn't work, see what else you can come up with, and even then don't accept that as 'your' way, or the next piece of stuff will catch you out. That is the joy of 'wood'; every piece is a challenge. Note – I may as well emphasise the fact that I do not generally use the term wood.

Drill driven lathes

As there must be hundreds of drill driven lathes about, I thought I would start with a few ideas for those who possess this type of lathe. There is one limitation to this equipment, and that is the ability to fit 'patent' chucks. Most will not accept these, but we can make our own. The production of this chuck will, I hope, open up a far greater range of projects that can be produced on the drill driven lathe, as the making of pepper mills is by no means its only use. The equipment here is ultra lightweight, produced by Wolfcraft, and the only alteration I have made to the standard production model is to replace the toolrest supplied with my own as I am more used to its shape. I believe clamping to a table places the lathe too low for the average worker, so I made a simple stand, both to bring it up to elbow height between centres, and to add the rigidity that the lathe must have. The stand is held in my bench vice.

In its basic form the pepper mill is an interesting project calling for skill, patience, and a modest understanding of mechanics. It works, it moves, and above all 'it does something', and is always an acceptable gift. One could write a big book on the various ways of producing mills, mainly due to the number of accessories that are available now. One of the most important is the stainless steel salt mechanism which will permit the manufacture of perfectly matching pairs. I would like to devote this chapter to a few variations that I hope will inspire the reader.

Fig. 16.1. On the left we have a perfectly normal or standard production, with the exception of the centre section which is glass; the timber is Grande Palisander. Next left is one in Andaman Padauk and Satinwood with solid ends and a laminated centrepiece; the retaining knob is also recessed in the 'capstan' in a wide rebate. I think this makes not only a variation but adds comfort in handling. Then with the same proprietary glass inserts a pair with Hornbeam base, inlaid, and you will no doubt recognise the 'spalted' beech capstans. The knobs are again recessed in very small holes.

Fig. 16.2. Made in Hakia with a 'reclaimed' insert, the painted label I leave intact for novelty effect, but a little paint stripper will soon remove it if you wish to do so. A very popular coffee grinder model which is not discussed in the text as it is identical in process to the candle holder in Chapter 12. The hole must, of course, allow the ground pepper to escape. This one is in English Walnut Juglans. Finally, a pair in Indian Ebony with a laminated centre of Sycamore.

Fig. 16.3.   As the faceplate is required for other projects from time to time, a piece of hardwood is mounted with bolts, the heads of which are well recessed and secured with epoxy. The hardwood disc is identified to the faceplate to enable it to be replaced in the same position after removal. Nuts and washers will make for greater security and permanency, and such jigs will have a long life. Several can be made of differing sizes.

Fig. 16.4.   Taking care not to foul or disturb the bolts retaining the hardwood disc and using the point of the long corner of a skew chisel, take only *light* cuts to produce the rebate. The power of this type of equipment comes mainly from its speed, about 3000rpm or a little more. Heavy cuts will slow down the drill, possibly damaging it, and will not help the working at all. For these reasons it is vital for accurate working that the tools be correctly shaped and kept very sharp.

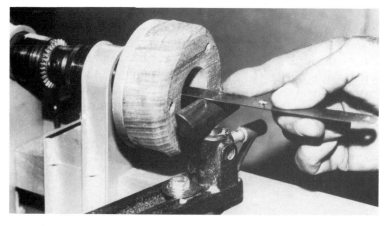

Fig. 16.5.   Take the time and trouble to ensure that the rebate, which will accept the dowel of the working part of the chuck, is both accurate in diameter and depth. Also ensure that the base of the rebate is flat and square with the sides, as this will not only increase the adhesive area but mechanically strengthen the chuck.

Fig. 16.6.   The standard roughing out gouge is a little 'hefty' to use on such lightweight equipment. I am using here a ⅜in spindle gouge, keeping the speed of the machine at maximum by taking light cuts to reduce the square down to a cylinder. It would of course be possible to take the corners off first with a hand plane, a practice I would actively discourage. If you get into this habit, what do you do when a profile with square ends such as a table leg is required. Don't be 'chicken' with square stuff. Approach the work with the handle of the gouge very low and let the bevel contact, rub, then gently lift the handle until a cut is felt and traverse the tool along the toolrest. That is all there is to it.

Fig. 16.7.   Even a jig or chuck that is home-made wants to be a credit to the maker and a pleasure to use, so a few finishing cuts with a sharp chisel will obviate a lot of sanding, and provide a bit of practice.

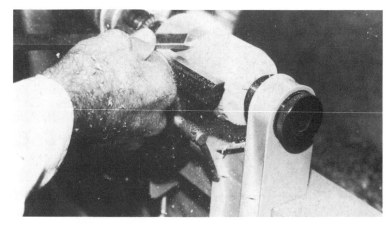

Fig. 16.8.   The dowel to fit the rebate worked in the faceplate can be produced on either end of the cylinder. The tailstock end is naturally preferable as it is free of the drive centre and/or drill chuck and the associated hazards. A parting tool will do this job to perfection with a succession of cuts, and leave a slightly roughened surface that will assist adhesion.

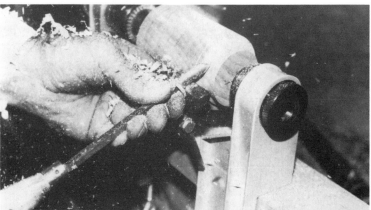

Fig. 16.9.   One of the basic principles of installing a lathe is to ensure it is free, or as free as you can make it, of vibration. Vibration is the curse of the woodturner. With a chuck such as this, used in a hefty lathe like mine, the imbalance occasioned by the screw section of a hoseclip would make little difference. However, with a light lathe such as we are discussing here *any* effort that can be made to reduce vibration will be a great asset to good turning. For this reason I have used two hoseclips made up as one, but there is no reason why three could not be employed. This also offers a more positive centring moment to the work held within the chuck, as each screw is tightened in turn to equalise both pressure and balance. Before working the opening of the chuck, assemble the hoseclips by opening them out and screwing the two, or three, back together as one of larger diameter. Place them on the workpiece and tighten securely, leave for a moment or two, and the assembly will have taken up its new shape accurately.

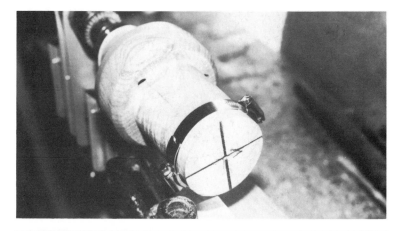

Fig. 16.10.   The chuck can now be worked to the size required, using the long corner of a skew, and to a depth of about 2in or less for this work. It will be realised that if the section we are working becomes worn or damaged, it can be cut off and there is enough length remaining to re-make if required. The same applies of course if a change of size is required. N.B. you can make the opening larger, you can't make it smaller. When the whole is finished with, it can be cut off and a new dowelled piece let into the faceplate piece. Now produce the four or more saw kerfs, guided by the heavy lines in Fig. 16.9.

Fig. 16.11. The workpiece is secured in the chuck. It can be pre-bored if necessary in the drillpress. The profiles for the base sections of the mechanism are now worked and a neat fit ensured, and completed in this mode.

Fig. 16.12. The workpiece is then reversed and the rebate to accept the glass, or laminated section, is produced. In practice a drillpress is unnecessary as one half of the hole could be worked as shown in Fig. 16.11 and the other half now. The sizing of glass to timbers wants to be 'easy', even a fraction sloppy as glass is inert, and timber will move. A silicone 'caulk' will have enough adhesive power to secure the glass centrepiece to the timber. The capstan is produced in like manner, or as we will discuss in a moment.

Fig. 16.13. The proprietary glass sections are most attractive, but cost money. An alternative is to produce our own from what would normally be thrown away. Glass, even pottery, containers come in a vast array of attractive styles. They are quite free so if the following takes a little practice it will cost nothing but your time and a minimal amount of gas. The idea is to use the top of the container, where the lid goes, to form the bearing surface for the capstan, so we must remove the base. Glass is nothing like as difficult to work as you might think, and when I was shown how to do this I realised just how easy it is. I also learned glass does not care for anything 'sudden', take your time. A file is used to score a line *complete and unbroken* around the base, about ⅛in above the thickness of the glass at the base, or more if you wish to shorten. A pencil flame is then played round this line, or vice versa as in this case. The tip only of the flame should touch the glass and, after a few seconds, a distinct 'click' will be audible. Remove from the heat source *at once*.

Fig. 16.14. In most cases the base will just fall off into your *gloved* hand. If it does not, a light tap on the bench will release it, and with practice (the cutting or scoring seems to be the most important) a neat cut will be effected.

Fig. 16.15. While the end we have been studying will be buried in the timber and needs no further attention, it is as well to tidy things up. A few rubs on a piece of very coarse garnet (80 grit or so) will not only indicate a caring attitude on the part of the maker, but also produce a roughened area for the adhesion.

Fig. 16.16. Reverting now to my own lathe to demonstrate another method, here was a pre-bored section in the square mounted on a home-made mandrel, on a screwchuck. It was then turned to a cylinder and the profile to accept a 'jar' glass insert produced.

Fig. 16.17. While straight sided inserts can be assembled with ease and accuracy, a tapered shape such as here is best supported with the tailstock for at least as long as the adhesive takes to set. This will ensure that the capstan or turret will turn true and be smooth running. I have used the actual lid of the jar here, but if this had not been available a piece of ply would suffice. A word of caution – we all develop habits in working, and one is to rest the hand on the workpiece to hasten stopping when the lathe is switched off. This may be fine in normal working, but some jigs or chucks will have projections, so resist the temptation. You will only do it once! Another is to give the work 'a spin' under power to polish off some specks or whatever. Do not in any circumstances use power to turn work that contains exposed glass; finish the timber completely then glue the insert.

Fig. 16.18. In common with most timbers Hornbeam can in some trees have a delightful figure, and such would be best left. This was not such a piece; it was plain and without interest. One way to produce a pleasing effect is to use an inlay banding, the sort that cabinet makers use. Such material comes in a wide variety of designs and widths, and is easily moulded around a diameter of 2¼in, such as we have here. First, the workpiece must be completely finished to size. It is not wise to try to turn bandings. The width of the inlay can be laid off on the stuff with a fine pencil.

Fig. 16.19. The rebate for the banding can be worked with a parting tool, carefully, and to a depth that will permit the banding to sit just the tiniest bit proud. A rule of thumb here is to work the rebate *exactly* to the thickness of the banding, allowing the adhesive thickness to provide the 'proudness' that will ensure a super flush finish when papered.

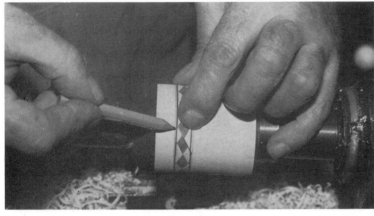

Fig. 16.20. Site the banding in the rebate and with a hard, fine-pointed pencil very lightly mark for sizing. Take the banding to a flat surface and cut just into the waste side of the pencil line.

Fig. 16.21. I find an impact adhesive is best for this work, if necessary. If you use a non impact adhesive, the banding can be held in place with elastic bands. Slide these bands onto the workpiece first and ensure they are tight, then slip them over the banding after rubbing down with the pein of a hammer as seen here.

Fig. 16.22. It is wise policy to have completed all the necessary fittings of inserts etc before tackling any inlay, but there is no rule on the subject, if for any reason you wish to do it the other way round. The work is reversed, again on a home-made mandrel, or pin chuck if you have one. Note the abraided end of the glass insert to the left of this figure. It only takes a moment with garnet and will ensure a permanent job.

Fig. 16.23.   A small mandrel made up on a screwchuck with two diameters for holding the piece of stuff for the capstan. The larger will be a snug fit to the turning or bearing area of the capstan, the smaller will fit the hole in which the drive disc is retained. Either would in practice be enough to support the workpiece, but both makes for certainty.

Fig. 16.24.   The headstock end of the capstan is completed then slipped onto the mandrel. The balance of the styling and the ³/₁₆in hole to accommodate the drive shaft can be pre-drilled if necessary or completed in this mode. The whole can now be finished and polished and, with this mandrel retained, the workpiece can be returned to the lathe as often as is required, for finishing.

Fig. 16.25.   Careful preparation of the laminates for the centre sections is essential. Most turnings will be handled or seen close-up, e.g. tableware which sits almost at eye level thoughout a meal. Any imperfections will be immediately visible and, for me anyway, become irritating. The four sections of Satinwood are prepared, face and edge, and clearly marked. Veneer can be used if available but I have prepared the thin ⅛in strips of Padauk myself. These strips are glued both sides and the cramps applied.

Fig. 16.26.   A locating mark should be made, as the 'V' seen here. This will ensure the work is returned to the same position each time a test for fitting the two halves together is made. When the area is perfectly flat, the second strip is inserted with adhesive and the cramps applied.

Fig. 16.27. The two large cramps will secure the two halves together and the small cramps will stop sideways slip. The strip in the halves *must* line up perfectly.

Fig. 16.28. The centre dictated by the veneer, or insert, must be used in favour of 'X' marking the work, thus it becomes self centring. If the facility for boring in the lathe is not available, the holes can be completed in the drillpress or even by hand with great care. If the latter method is employed it is best to work from both ends. A short mandrel, one that is short of the halfway mark, will then compensate for any inaccuracy in drilling by hand when the work is mounted up for turning.

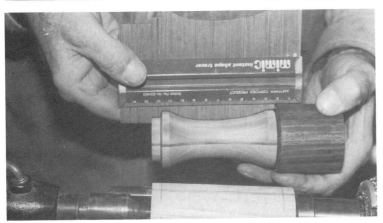

Fig. 16.29. The centrepiece is made as a separate piece, in effect as the glass inserts are. The base and capstan we have covered. With the first of the pair completed a template can be formed to produce the mate. Make sure the template has a reference point, indicated here at my left hand. Provided this is maintained in the exact square position when working the mate, reproduction will be a true replica. It may be of interest to readers who find repetition a little difficult that so long as the overall height, and general girth is satisfactory, little errors in detail have to be looked for very hard.

Combined techniques

Fig. 17.1.   This Chapter is a 'bringing together' of some of the techniques we have been looking at, and at the same time, will give us the opportunity to discuss a few other methods of securing work for the various processes required. We can study a few other jigs at the same time. While this project is a smoker's companion, and the spare length of stave, which it is always wise to provide, was used to make a matching ashtray, the variations will be obvious. For instance, a lady's sewing basket complete with dowels to hold the reels of cotton. You can even use a 'lazy susan' bearing and place the whole on a stand. The timber here is Cuban Mahogany, Swetinia Mahogoni. I believe it is from Cuba or thereabouts, but sometimes importers are a little

secretive about the source of their supplies. It is a delightful timber, of mahogany style and yellowish when first worked, but deepening to a rich red on exposure to ultra violet light. Soft to work, it takes a fine finish. Being a tobacco container, the lid must be airtight, and for this, the fitting will be covered. Washers are available in packets from hardware stores, and are in effect preserving jar rings. By making your own cutting template they can also be made from sheet *food quality* rubber. Do not use neoprin as this will taint the contents of the container. The finish used in this project was Danish oil, outside; the inside is lined. Five coats were applied in accordance with the maker's instructions, and while this is a time consuming finish and a 'sticky' job, I like it very much. Applied with a rag (stored between coats in a tin), it is simple, economic, and durable. As each application is wiped dry after about ten minutes, there will be no nibs to mar the finish and no brushmarks or rings either.

Fig. 17.2.   With a multi section project like this one has to start somewhere, so let us dispose of the knob first. With the stuff mounted on a screwchuck and supported by the tailstock (in which is a revolving centre), the work is reduced to a cylinder with a roughing out gouge or similar.

Fig. 17.3.   When the style is almost complete the tailstock can be withdrawn, and as a flat, or nearly flat, top was required, a slice or two across with a chisel will leave a perfect finish to the endgrain. As this is one of those cuts that can skid and spoil the work, I always leave a safety factor. If a skid occurs, you will be able to remove the mark when the knob is finally styled.

Fig. 17.4.   The dowel is produced to accommodate a drill size and to the required length. A few rings produced with a chisel or parting tool will aid adhesion.

Fig. 17.5.   As the knob on this sort of project will receive considerable use during its life, I feel a pre-build up of friction polish is a good idea. The Danish oil takes on it with no difficulty.

Fig. 17.6.   The part of the lid that will both centre the jar and contain the airtight washer wants to be ¹⁄₁₆in under the size of the opening of the jar. This will make for ease in use and prevent misalignment of the lid when finished. In effect, this whole area is to some extent governed by the size of the washer available, and this will vary.

Fig. 17.7.   The slot to contain the washer must be produced to the exact size of the i.d. of the washer. Thus it will be completely sealed at this point; if loose it will tend to become dislodged in use. The slot is worked with a parting tool of a width to match the washer thickness, to render an easy but not sloppy fit.

Fig. 17.8.   The styling or shaping of the lid can now be completed with a gouge.

Fig. 17.9.   Alternatively, a scraper can be employed if the timber used will accept it. Always point a scraper *downwards* as shown, *never* upwards. N.B. It is an extremely dangerous practice to make scrapers from old files – tool steel, professionally made for the purpose will preserve your safety.

Fig. 17.10.   The hole to accept the knob can now be drilled, dead centre, with a chuck fitted to the tailstock. Take care not to foul the screw in the screwchuck. If the workpiece is thin, start the hole as shown and finish off in the drillpress.

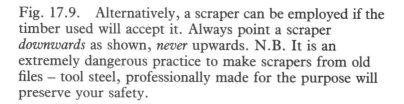

Fig. 17.11. As we will be making this insert captive and fitting from the base, we can make use of the template discussed in Fig. 2.39. The base of this insert is tapered, not flush with the side. A piece of spare stuff is used to mark the true base and the flange is produced to this mark. This action will ensure an insert that is snug fitting.

Fig. 17.12. With the lining inserted and the base piece worked to size, the lathe can be used as a cramp overnight or, in any of the ways we have discussed, to glue the base which in this instance is fitted flush.

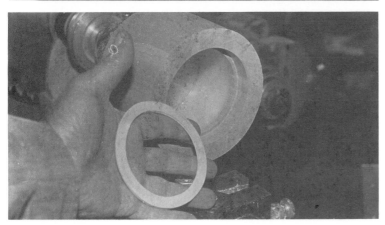

Fig. 17.13. For an airtight, but easy-for-use, fit to this type of work I size the opening to just a fraction less, $\frac{1}{64}$in or less of the o.d. of the washer. By the time the opening is sanded, and finished, a perfect 'hiss fit' can be obtained. Still retaining the faceplate, the work is removed from the lathe for the next operation. The faceplate remains in this position throughout this project.

Fig. 17.14. As in Figs. 4.28 to 4.31, the base of this project is centred in the 'Boulter jig' and the centre is worked to the desired size. As long as the jig is not badly knocked about with use, a small square can be used to ensure the flange worked is completely square.

Fig. 17.15.   As we will see in a moment the immediate area around the centre will, to say the least, be difficult to get at later, so it is as well to finish, even sand at this time. Take great care not to foul the grips.

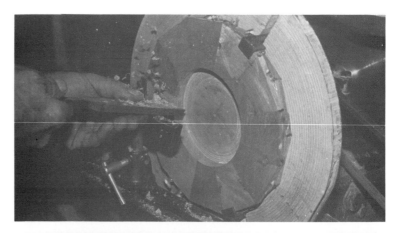

Fig. 17.16.   As it will not be possible to slide the base piece over the work to test for fit, I lay it over the headstock as shown here. The alternative would be to remove the workpiece from the lathe several times to ensure a snug fitting base.

Fig. 17.17.   The base piece fitted, it is now time to work any styling required to the jar, before this is glued in place. Remove any glue squeeze with a damp cloth and render this area clean and tidy after the adhesive is applied. It will be tedious to get at later during finishing.

Fig. 17.18.   As the work is supported by the base of the jar, when the adhesive holding the basepiece is set (overnight) work can commence on shaping. The irregular outside is turned first, and any styling completed.

Fig. 17.19.   Then the toolrest can be brought round to complete the necessary work, in this case a hollow to confine the bowls of pipes. Worked here with a gouge, then in the next figure finished with a domed scraper.

Fig. 17.20.   It will now be seen how vexing it could have been to have to work, even sand, right up to the corner where the jar meets the base. The jar will have been sanded, finishing with hand sanding *with the grain*, and this would be spoiled if, of necessity, the base must be sanded at right angles to it.

Fig. 17.21.   For the 'stem ring', the top ring that holds the stem of the pipe, we must look at another method of holding work that has no centre. Small pieces of hardwood are prepared with a slot, a panel pin driven into the end is nipped off at an angle to form a point, or filed to shape. These are mounted on a disc of stuff, ply in this case, that will very snugly fit the i.d. worked as previously discussed in the workpiece.

Fig. 17.22.   On a perfectly flat surface the workpiece is pressed onto the disc and the hardwood 'drive pins' are then tapped into the workpiece and secured with the woodscrew. While a normal faceplate or screwchuck could be used, I prefer to employ the setscrew method, as this means I can remove the workpiece without the tedium of a faceplate getting in the way of other operations. We now have a 'centreless' ring that can be worked to a complete finish if required. We, of course, are not going to do anything as simple as that! However, the periphery must be turned both true and preferably square for the next operation.

Fig. 17.23. It is never an easy task to produce holes round the periphery of turned work freehand, thus some form of guide or jig must be devised. This one is simplicity itself, a piece of chipboard with two dowels set approx 6in or so apart, but this dimension will depend entirely on the size of work. The dowels are equidistant from the back of the board and a heavy pencil line is drawn dead centre at right angles to the rear. It is then necessary to position the board on the drillpress table to permit the centre of the drill to strike the pencil line. It follows that anything circular that is secured within the triangle thus formed must be worked equally and accurately. The only other measurement that has to be determined is where on the workpiece the hole is required, and this can be adjusted by moving the board back or forward.

Fig. 17.24. The other consideration is the number of holes, which depends on the project. By adjusting the board as described and drilling through each joint of one layer of lamination the hole was produced dead centre of the other. Thus 12 holes were produced perfectly spaced with no measuring required. All the work was kept under complete control and hand held.

Fig. 17.25. To avoid spelching it is as well not to drill the holes right though, as the further shaping will reveal them. The periphery of the holes will be neat and fine. The workpiece can now be returned to the lathe for final working and, held in the chuck in this way, can be reversed if necessary.

Fig. 17.26.   Final turning of the periphery using a wide beading tool. The work can now be sanded and polished, if required, and removed from the disc.

Fig. 17.27.   The finished piece of section with the holes for the pipe stems drilled equidistant in all directions, dead centre of each of the 12 segments, with no measuring necessary. Clever, isn't it?

Fig. 17.28.   The stem ring can now be glued to the top of the project and any further adjustment made if required. The masking tape will prevent accidental damage to the finished jar if any further sanding is necessary, but for obvious reasons this should be avoided if at all possible.

Lace bobbins

The origin of the craft of bobbin or pillow lace making is the subject of much controversy, but it has been much in evidence since the 15th century. Today there are a few, if any, professional lace makers. A nine inch square handkerchief with a two inch fine lace border could take one hundred hours to produce, even for an accomplished crafts lady. If you compare this to the charge for labour your local garage would make for a hundred hours of work on your car, such a product would be, to say the least, uncommercial. That said, the craft is flourishing, and clubs are proliferating, formed by enthusiasts purely for the pleasure of the members, to ensure the survival of the craft, and to enjoy what must be the great satisfaction of its mastery. Commercially-made bobbins are available, in aluminium, plastic and even in wood. They are as inexpensive as they are 'ordinary', and their use is confined to beginners, and those who are unable to obtain the hand-made bobbin that the experienced lace maker covets. As with all crafts, as one's skill improves, more and better tools are required. This fact of course opens the door for the woodturner, and to my certain knowledge there are many 'home craftsmen' and indeed ladies, who enjoy a profitable pastime making exquisite bobbins and offering them for sale at 'lace days', as the exhibitions of the craft are known. I am much indebted to my friend Richard Tomalin, an intrepid bobbin maker, who kindly permitted me to photograph him at work. A visit to a 'lace day' will be found rewarding to anyone interested in craft in its finest form, and would help towards an understanding of what the lace maker requires, and to discover some of the tradition and folklore in which the craft abounds. There are many types and sizes of bobbin, and although some are named geographically, it is a reference to a method rather than to where in particular a lace is made. Most bobbins have a spangle of usually seven beads; Honiton bobbins do not. Different shapes and decoration are given specific names like 'Leopard', or 'Bucks Point'. Furthermore, lace makers require bobbins for commemorative purposes, like weddings, births, Christmas, anniversaries etc, and these quite obviously can only be provided by a woodturner.

The timbers used in bobbin making need to be, for the finer bobbins, of hardwood. Beware of some of the dyewoods, i.e. some dalbergias will 'bleed' and this will discolour the cotton. For the less expensive bobbins, fruitwoods are ideal. In fact, pearwood is one of the standard timbers used. It will be found, in general, that lace makers are very interested in what their bobbins are made

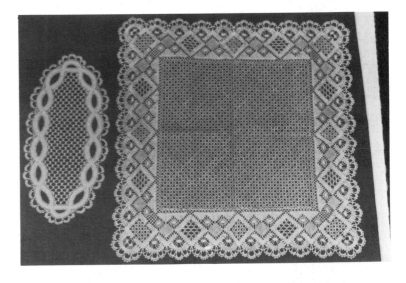

of, where the timber comes from, and its botanical reference. While this chapter covers the basic techniques of bobbin manufacture, as the turner will often wish to make small delicate pieces, and as we will be making our first bobbin from bone and not from timber, this will open up a new dimension. I'm sure this will give food for thought, especially for the model maker or those interested in miniature work in general.

The bone we will be using is easily obtained from the butcher. It's beef 'shinbone' from the forequarter and is prepared as follows. With a little water in the bottom of a pressure cooker, boil for about two hours according to size. It is not necessary to buy the biggest bone you can find, as a starting size of material approx 5/16in square will be ample. Allow the bone to dry thoroughly. You will, of course, have cut it up into lengths of approx 4½in before boiling, and it can now be cut into convenient strips for working. Bobbin makers have various methods of working or supporting the workpiece. Richard likes to use his home-made drive centre, which is of timber. A morse taper is produced as normal between-centres work, inserted into the drive mandrel of the lathe and a convenient size hole bored, about ¼in diameter. This hole is then very carefully squared to accept square or rough squared stuff, thus anything that is turned in the home-made drive will automatically become symmetrical when reduced to a cylinder. Other methods would be to use a tapered 'pin mandrel' (of Coronet pattern) or an engineer's geared chuck. Some, of course, will use a normal drive centre, but it will be obvious that no great pressure must be applied.

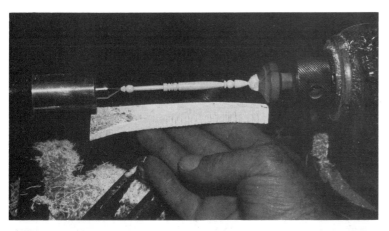

Fig. 18.1.   A finished bone bobbin and the raw material from which the next will be produced. The irregular shape of the bone need not be a problem, as the drive end can be rough squared on the bandsaw in a slightly tapered form to fit the square format of the drive centre. Alternatively, if using a pin mandrel (which is manufactured with a tapered hollow centre by Coronet) no further shaping of the stuff will be necessary after cutting to rough square form. Those who use an engineer's geared chuck will perhaps need to reduce the stuff to cylinder form, as normal between-centres work, before inserting into the engineer's chuck.

Fig. 18.2.   Bone works in much the same way as timber and no special tools, angle of grind or techniques, are necessary. No undue dulling of tool edges will be found. A standard roughing gouge will be found an ideal tool to quickly reduce the stuff to cylindrical form, and to a diameter of about ¼in fine. The tailstock end is worked first, progressing towards the drive centre.

Fig. 18.3.   The chisel will remove any slight tears occasioned by the use of the roughing gouge, and is used to reduce the stuff down to within a fraction of the finished diameter, a little less than ¼in in this case. Richard is here working from left to right, and it is interesting to note how high or near to the long corner of the skew chisel he is working. Due to the tiny diameter of the workpiece, the chisel is presented almost square to the work and is almost flat on the toolrest. All this would not be the 'norm' in general woodturning.

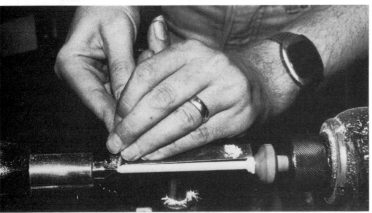

Fig. 18.4.   As the pressure of the tailstock must be very light, just enough to support the work, there will be only the slightest indent in the end of the workpiece and this is left visible in the finished bobbin. The area worked first is called the 'short neck', which is the part of the bobbin where the cotton is temporarily knotted. Different bobbin makers have their own particular designs. It is, of course, imperative for the lace maker that the bobbin is completely smooth and free from any snags, but as we will see in a moment, it is equally important in finishing the bobbin that it be so. It is for this reason that, as each section is worked, it is completed as smooth as possible with the tool, as the very minimum of sanding due to the fragility of the finished piece will be required.

Fig. 18.5.   The 'long neck', the part of the bobbin around which the cotton is wound, is the next to be completed. While it is common practice to support thin work with the fingers, it is more usual to see the hand over the work. However, such support gives complete control, and as the speed only needs to be between 1000 and 1500rpm, no undue heating of the fingertips will be noticed. This was a normal size chisel but is held as shown for complete control. The area of the long neck is scribed by the point of the chisel, and then reduced with cuts from alternate directions. More of this in a moment.

Fig. 18.6.   Any further decoration or detail on the tailstock end of the barrel of the bobbin should be completed while there is some thickness to the stuff to support such cuts. Note that in all the following the tool is controlled with the fingers of the right hand and the thumb of the left, leaving the fingers of the left hand free to support the work.

Fig. 18.7.   Returning to the long neck with successive passes to the left and right, this section is reduced to a diameter of about ⅛in.

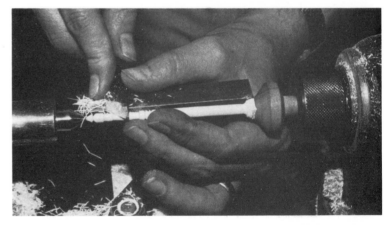

Fig. 18.8.   When working toward the supporting finger, take care not to pass the chisel through the top of your fingers! At this stage, concentration should be at maximum.

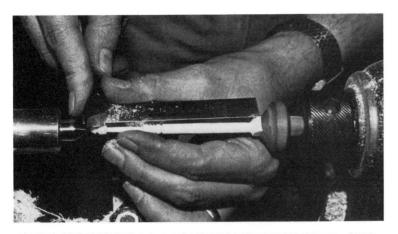

Fig. 18.9.   With the long neck finished, there will be room to complete the short neck. This is done using the short corner of the chisel, much in the same way as working a bead.

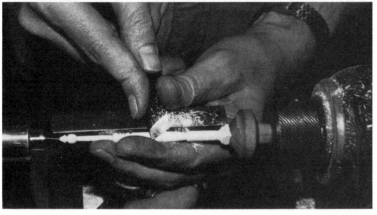

Fig. 18.10.   When the tailstock half of the bobbin is worked to as near completion as is possible, the barrel area can be started. While the tip of the chisel appears to be very close to the finger in this figure, and indeed it is to some extent, it is necessary to support the work as shown. In this area whip is most likely to occur, and such would probably snap the work at its weakest point.

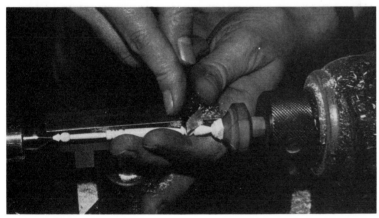

Fig. 18.11.   The remainder of the decoration detail (according to the particular style of the maker or the requirements of the user) are completed. Progressive cuts are made to diminish the size of the stuff ready for a final cut to sever. Now is the time to apply some very fine garnet abrasive to smooth, followed by steel wool. Take care the steel wool does not wrap round the bobbin. Some makers drill the fine hole, no larger than ¹⁄₆₄in diameter for the wire on which the 'spangle' beads are attached; others complete this operation in a jig after felling off.

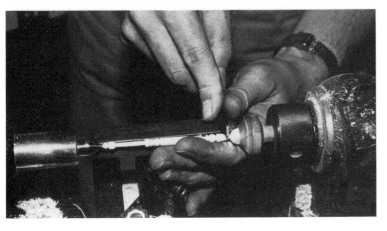

Fig. 18.12.   With some hardwoods the finish can be obtained with nothing more than a really good quality household furniture polish ('Renaissance' Wax is excellent). However, very carefully applied friction polish would be used for such as fruitwoods. The final parting off, which to save further hand finishing, needs to be as clean as possible. Place the chisel, long corner up, and in a bevel rubbing but not cutting position to establish contact with the revolving workpiece. With the lightest of pressure, using only the short corner of the tool, gently push it into the thin part to completely sever and leave a smooth tooled finish. Bobbins made from timber are completed in exactly the same way as this one in bone, but for obvious reasons it is advisable to start with a hardwood, which will tolerate more severe working, until experience is gained.

Fig. 18.13. Lace makers like to have a wide variety of different timbers and styles. I would imagine this is a help in identifying the pairs in working, but I suspect that it is also due to interest in the timber from which bobbins are made. One such variation is known as a 'jingle'. It's a normal bobbin as we have discussed, but has a loose bead at the spangle end. I felt it well worth inclusion here as again, for the miniature worker, the method will present many variations.

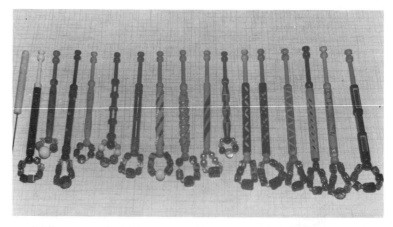

Fig. 18.14. A bead is worked in the usual way but a little extra waste is removed from either side to permit the hook-shaped tool to enter the base of the bead to under cut, shape and finally separate from the body of the bobbin.

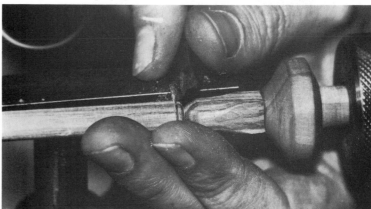

Fig. 18.15. Still using the home-made drive centre (in these close-up photos its application can be seen to advantage), it will be obvious that if you cut your own blanks the size can match the drive centre. The bead is completed with straight sides and a little deeper than would be normal, as this allows plenty of room for the further operation.

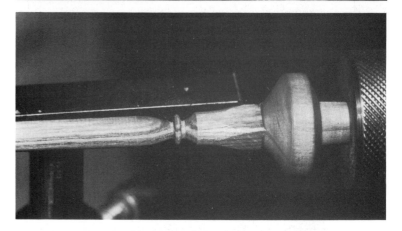

Fig. 18.16. The hook-shaped tool used here is home-made by Richard from a HSS (high speed steel) hacksaw blade, ground and shaped to a configuration very much like a linoleum knife. Special attention is paid to the tip or point (which is the only part used). A word of caution here, HSS is excellent for hacksaws but is very brittle and not really suitable for this sort of work. However, there is always the exception to any rule, and as the strain on this particular tool is minimal it is perhaps, acceptable. Nevertheless it would be prudent to wear a facemask, just in case. I would advise strongly against ever making tools from any steel that is not produced for specific wood working.

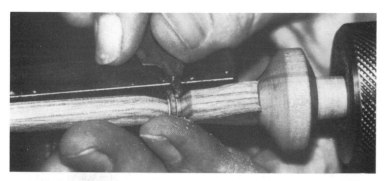

Fig. 18.17. The special tool is worked very gently into the base of the bead, from each side a little at a time.

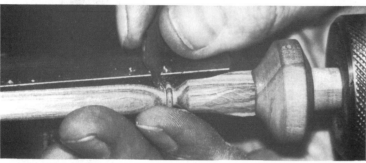

Fig. 18.18. Working the shape of the underside of the bead to conform with the top. When most of the waste is removed, a light sanding all round (as much as you can get at) can be completed. When all is smooth, the 'ring' can be separated with a cut from both sides.

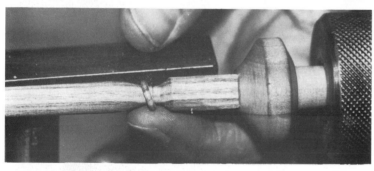

Fig. 18.19. It is not necessary to effect a fine finish on the body of the bobbin as this can be worked later. The main thing to remember is to effect the best shape or finish on the loose bead/ring while it is attached to the workpiece. No working will be possible once it is separated. Here the ring is separated and there is enough waste removed from both sides to allow it to be pushed out of the way as the remainder of the working is completed.

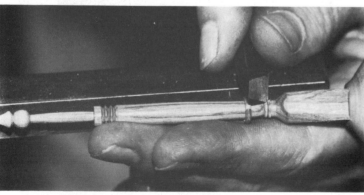

Fig. 18.20. With the ring pushed along the barrel out of the working area and held in this position with the finger, the area where the ring was separated can be cleaned up and further shaped. The ring will of course be delicate, therefore no undue force should be applied to jam it on the taper shape.

Fig. 18.21. The completed 'jingle' bobbin is then finished and polished, with a final cut to sever and leave a clean end. At all times it is supported by the fingers.

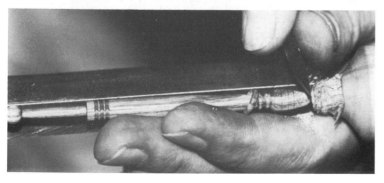

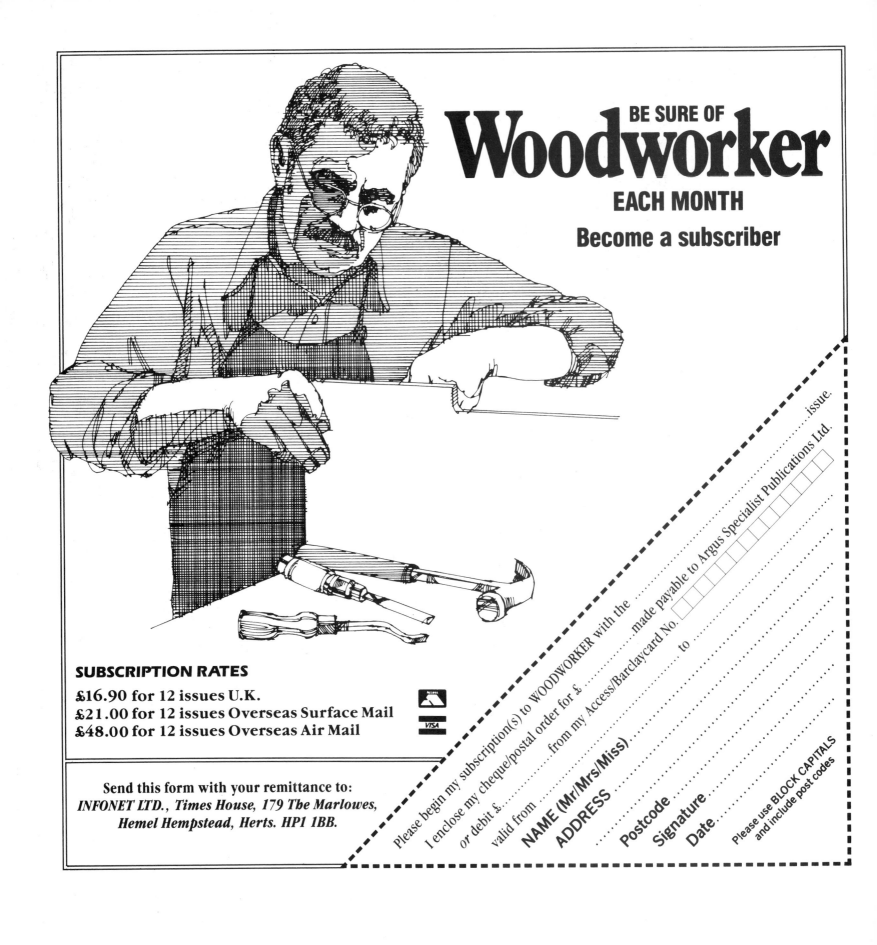